AMC 8 Practice Tests
Volume 1

AlphaStar Academy
Math Development Team

Adam Tang, Alex Gu, Edwin Xie,
Gavin Yu, Jonathan Huang, Kelly Cui,
Stephen Xia, Suhas Kotha, Tiger Che,
and Ali Gurel

About AlphaStar Academy Math Development Team

AlphaStar Academy is an education company based in Bay Area, California. It offers extensive training programs for gifted students towards national and international Math and Science competitions such as American Mathematics Competitions, MathCounts, USA Math Olympiads, USA Computing Olympiads, and F=ma:

https://alphastar.academy/

Students and teams from AlphaStar Academy performed extremely well in Mathematics Competitions and Olympiads, with countless of students finishing in top 10 and teams finishing in first place in competitions including Harvard-MIT Math Tournament, Princeton Math Competition, Stanford Math Tournament, Berkeley Math Tournament, and Caltech Harvey Mudd Math Competition. Dozens of AlphaStar Academy students got perfect scores in AMC 8/10/12 over the years and most of the MathCounts California team members in recent years were AlphaStar students. Moreover, every year between 2017 and 2020, at least one of the six-member USA IMO team was an AlphaStar Academy student/alumni.

Starting 2020, AlphaStar Academy has started offering all of its courses and programs online.

This book contains four AMC 8 practice exams with new problems not from any past competitions and with insightful solutions. It is written by AlphaStar Math Development Team, a group of expert students and alumni of AlphaStar Academy, who have participated and got excellent results in these competitions.

Team members and authors of this book in alphabetical order are Adam Tang, Alex Gu, Edwin Xie, Gavin Yu, Jonathan Huang, Kelly Cui, Stephen Xia, Suhas Kotha, and Tiger Che. They have had tremendous success in Math Competitions themselves. In particular, in AMC 8, the authors had a combined number of 6 Perfect scores and 21 Distinguished Honor Roll Awards which is given to only top 1% of participants each year.

The team was guided by Dr. Ali Gurel who also did the editing. Dr. Gurel has a PhD in Mathematics with emphasis on Number Theory from California Institute of Technology. He was a former mathlete himself, earning a Silver Medal in the International Mathematics Olympiads (IMO), highest level of math competition for high school students. In 2007, he received the Scott Russell Johnson Prize for Excellence in Graduate Teaching from Caltech. He served as an Advisory Panel Member for the American Mathematics Competitions between 2008 and 2012, and taught at USA Math Olympiad Summer Program (MOSP) between 2007 and 2012, a three-week program where top students in USA including the USA IMO team are trained. He has coached gifted students and teams for more than two decades and dozens of his students won Gold, Silver, Bronze medals at the International Math Olympiads. He is one of the founders and the Math Director of the AlphaStar Academy.

To The Reader

The American Mathematics Competition 8 (AMC 8) is a twenty-five question multiple choice test that is taken in USA and many other countries by tens of thousands of middle-school and sometimes elementary school students. The questions do not stray far from the curriculum of what is covered in school. However instead of being straight-forward, most questions require a deeper level of thought to solve than ordinary textbook problems.

As such, one of the best ways to get better at Math contests similar to AMC 8 is to build intuition with lots of practice using various types of problems.

Do not be disheartened by the difficulty of the problems. Building skill takes time, and these problems are meant to be difficult. For example, in 2019, the average score was approximately 10, and only 25% of students scored over 12 points, which is less than half the total possible score. Furthermore, since the overall difficulty of the contest tends to increase over the years, we have intended these practice tests to be a little more difficult than what we expect the actual contest to be in the following years.

Additionally, to succeed on the test, it is crucial to be able to manage your time well. Not only should these tests serve as a text of problems but also as a tool to simulate an actual testing environment. Press yourself to finish with extra time to spare, but if time runs out, keep solving, and see how much time it takes. Try to gradually reduce your time over tests. Check your work for mistakes. Sometimes it can be a mistake as simple as switching from positive to negative. Be careful not losing the easy points. A hard-earned point by spending 5 minutes on the last problem on the test gives you the same credit as the easiest problem on the test. Remember: Everyone makes mistakes, but the best test solvers are those who learn from their mistakes.

In the official contest, there is no penalty for guessing so make sure to give an answer to each question. For these practice tests, you should continue solving problems past the time limit and look at the answers and solutions only after attempting all of the problems in a test.

To make the most out of this book, you should learn from the solutions presented, and most importantly, you should focus on developing a mathematical intuition. To do well in these contests, it is essential to develop an *intuition* for the problems. This is something you can only acquire by getting your hands dirty and working on problems that are just out of your reach. We hope that this book will give you the perfect sandbox to explore various ideas and eventually figure out how to come up with beautiful solutions to complex problems. Remember, Math doesn't have to be all about work. Every problem is a puzzle, so don't forget to have fun!

Table of Contents

AMC 8 PRACTICE TESTS VOL 1

TEST-1

INSTRUCTIONS

1. This is a twenty-five question multiple choice test. Each question is followed by answers marked A, B, C, D and E. Only one of these is correct.

2. There is no penalty for guessing. Your score is the number of correct answers.

3. Only scratch paper, graph paper, rulers, protractors, and erasers are allowed as aids. Calculators are NOT allowed. No problems on the test *require* the use of a calculator.

4. Figures are not necessarily drawn to scale.

5. You will have **40 minutes** to complete the test.

2

1. Evaluate $\dfrac{1}{2} + \dfrac{2}{3}$.

   (A) $\dfrac{3}{5}$ (B) 1   (C) $\dfrac{7}{6}$ (D) $\dfrac{5}{4}$ (E) $\dfrac{4}{3}$

2. Which of the following expressions is the largest?

   (A) $1+1+1+1+1$
   (B) $1+(1+1)\times 1+1$
   (C) $1+1\times 1\times 1+1$
   (D) $(1+1)\times 1\times(1+1)$
   (E) $1+1\times 1+1\times 1$

3. Steve begins with the number 5 and Taylor begins with the number 1. Every second, Steve doubles his number and Taylor triples her number. After how many seconds will Taylor's number be greater than Steve's number for the first time?

   (A) 3   (B) 4   (C) 5   (D) 6   (E) 7

4. Mimi has a box that contains two white socks, three black socks, five blue socks, and eight yellow socks. What is the minimum number of socks she must take out of the box to guarantee that she picked at least two socks with the same color?

   (A) 2   (B) 3   (C) 5   (D) 8   (E) 9

5. What is the side length of a square whose area is the same as the area of a unit circle?

   (A) 1   (B) $\dfrac{\sqrt{\pi}}{2}$ (C) $\sqrt{\dfrac{\pi}{2}}$ (D) $\sqrt{\pi}$ (E) $\sqrt{2\pi}$

6. 5 bops is equal to 20 gops and 3 gops is equal to 7 dops. How many bops is equal to 56 dops?

   (A) 3   (B) 4   (C) 5   (D) 6   (E) 8

7. In a geometric sequence, the second term is 3 and the seventh term is 96. What is the fifth term of this sequence?

   (A) 12   **(B)** 18   **(C)** 24   **(D)** 30   **(E)** 36

8. How many 4-digit numbers are divisible by 5 and only contain even digits?

   (A) 100   **(B)** 120   **(C)** 125   **(D)** 150   **(E)** 200

9. When an upward escalator is not working Alice can walk down in half a minute, using 60 steps. When she stands at the top and the escalator is moving she counts 75 steps of the escalator going by every minute. How many seconds will it take Alice to walk down the moving escalator?

   (A) 45   **(B)** 60   **(C)** 75   **(D)** 80   **(E)** 90

10. In a bag, there are six marbles: four red and two green. Bob starts randomly drawing marbles from the bag one at a time without replacement. What is the probability that the third marble he draws is green?

    (A) $\dfrac{1}{6}$ **(B)** $\dfrac{1}{3}$ **(C)** $\dfrac{1}{2}$ **(D)** $\dfrac{2}{3}$ **(E)** $\dfrac{5}{6}$

11. How many of the elements in $\{-2020, -2019, \ldots, 2019, 2020\}$ are perfect squares?

    (A) 44   **(B)** 45   **(C)** 88   **(D)** 89   **(E)** 90

12. What is the largest divisor of 210 that has no prime factor larger than 6?

    (A) 30   **(B)** 45   **(C)** 60   **(D)** 105   **(E)** 210

13. At Alpha Middle School, 60% of the students like swimming and 40% of the students like dancing. Among the students who like swimming, 20% like dancing. What percent of the people who like dancing do not like swimming?

(A) 30%   (B) 40%   (C) 50%   (D) 60%   (E) 70%

14. A triangle has side lengths 8, 15, and 17. What is the length of the shortest altitude of the triangle?

(A) $\dfrac{60}{17}$ (B) $\dfrac{35}{8}$ (C) $\dfrac{120}{17}$ (D) 8   (E) $\dfrac{35}{4}$

15. How many ordered triples (x, y, z) of distinct integers are there satisfying

$$(x - y)z = 4\left(\frac{1}{x} - \frac{1}{y}\right)?$$

(A) 12   (B) 18   (C) 21   (D) 24   (E) 48

16. The bottom of a pendulum, instead of swinging side to side, moves in a circular path while the string traces out the lateral face of a cone. If the length of the string holding the pendulum is 13 meters, and the length of one circular path is 10π meters, what is the volume of this cone, in cubic meters?

(A) 50π (B) 75π (C) 100π (D) 120π (E) 150π

17. Two real numbers satisfy the following properties:
    (a) when they are both increased by 5, their product doubles, and
    (b) when they are both decreased by 3, their product halves.
    What is the product when the two real numbers are both increased by 2?

(A) 300   (B) 330   (C) 360   (D) 390   (E) 420

18. A round table has five chairs labeled 1 through 5. How many ways are there for three girls and two boys to sit around the table, if the two boys may not sit next to each other?

    (A) 5   **(B)** 10   **(C)** 12   **(D)** 30   **(E)** 60

19. Out of the regular polygons with at most 100 sides, how many have interior angles that are integers when measured in degrees?

    (A) 18   **(B)** 19   **(C)** 20   **(D)** 21   **(E)** 22

20. In the diagram below, each of the four unit circles is tangent to two other circles, and the diagram is identical after a 90 degree rotation around its center. What is the area of the shaded region?

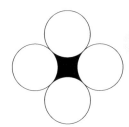

    (A) $1 - \dfrac{\pi}{4}$ **(B)** $2 - \dfrac{\pi}{2}$ **(C)** $\dfrac{3}{4}$ **(D)** $\dfrac{\pi}{4}$ **(E)** $4 - \pi$

21. What is the probability that a randomly chosen positive factor of 60^{60} is odd?

    (A) $\dfrac{1}{121}$ **(B)** $\dfrac{1}{120}$ **(C)** $\dfrac{1}{61}$ **(D)** $\dfrac{1}{60}$ **(E)** $\dfrac{1}{2}$

22. What is the remainder when 2^{8888} is divided by 18?

    (A) 2   **(B)** 4   **(C)** 8   **(D)** 10   **(E)** 14

23. Random Richard constructs a right triangle with two legs with length each chosen uniformly at random from the interval $(0, 2)$. To the nearest hundredth, what is the probability that the hypotenuse of Richard's triangle is greater than 2?

    (A) 0.21   **(B)** 0.23   **(C)** 0.25   **(D)** 0.27   **(E)** 0.29

24. Justin has a whiteboard with the integers from 5 to 20 written:

    $$5, 6, 7, \ldots, 20.$$

    Every minute, he chooses two of the numbers a and b on the board, erases them and writes $a + b - 10$ instead. He stops when there is only one number on the board. To his surprise, after trying this process many times, he always ends up with the same number. What is this number?

    (A) 25   **(B)** 50   **(C)** 100   **(D)** 150   **(E)** 200

25. In trapezoid $ABCD$, $AB \parallel CD$, $AB = 1$, and $CD = 3$. Lines $\overline{DA}$ and $\overline{CB}$ intersect at point P, and the area of triangle PDB is 6. What is the area of trapezoid $ABCD$?

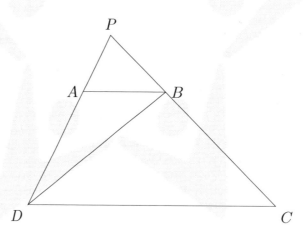

    (A) 12   **(B)** 14   **(C)** 15   **(D)** 16   **(E)** 18

Test-1 Answer Key

1. C
2. A
3. B
4. C
5. D
6. D
7. C
8. A
9. D
10. B
11. B
12. A
13. E
14. C
15. A
16. C
17. B
18. E
19. B
20. E
21. A
22. B
23. A
24. B
25. D

Test-1 Solutions

1. Evaluate $\dfrac{1}{2} + \dfrac{2}{3}$.

   (A) $\dfrac{3}{5}$ (B) 1 (C) $\dfrac{7}{6}$ (D) $\dfrac{5}{4}$ (E) $\dfrac{4}{3}$

   Answer (C):
   $$\frac{1}{2} + \frac{2}{3} = \frac{3}{6} + \frac{4}{6} = \frac{7}{6}.$$

2. Which of the following expressions is the largest?

   (A) $1 + 1 + 1 + 1 + 1$
   (B) $1 + (1 + 1) \times 1 + 1$
   (C) $1 + 1 \times 1 \times 1 + 1$
   (D) $(1 + 1) \times 1 \times (1 + 1)$
   (E) $1 + 1 \times 1 + 1 \times 1$

   Answer (A): We can evaluate each of these:
   (A) obviously evaluates to 5,
   (B) is equal to $1 + 2 + 1 = 4$,
   (C) is equal to $1 + 1 + 1 = 3$,
   (D) is equal to $2 \times 1 \times 2 = 4$, and
   (E) is equal to $1 + 1 + 1 = 3$.
   Therefore, the largest expression is (A).

3. Steve begins with the number 5 and Taylor begins with the number 1. Every second, Steve doubles his number and Taylor triples her number. After how many seconds will

11

Taylor's number be greater than Steve's number for the first time?

(A) 3 **(B)** 4 **(C)** 5 **(D)** 6 **(E)** 7

Answer (B): We can calculate Steve's and Taylor's numbers after every second:

seconds	0	1	2	3	4
Steve	5	10	20	40	80
Taylor	1	3	9	27	81

Taylor's number first surpasses Steve's number after 4 seconds.

4. Mimi has a box that contains two white socks, three black socks, five blue socks, and eight yellow socks. What is the minimum number of socks she must take out of the box to guarantee that she picked at least two socks with the same color?

(A) 2 **(B)** 3 **(C)** 5 **(D)** 8 **(E)** 9

Answer (C): Since there are only four colors, if we choose four socks, they could end up being all different colors. However, choosing 5 socks would ensure that there are at least two with the same color.

5. What is the side length of a square whose area is the same as the area of a unit circle?

(A) 1 **(B)** $\dfrac{\sqrt{\pi}}{2}$ **(C)** $\sqrt{\dfrac{\pi}{2}}$ **(D)** $\sqrt{\pi}$ **(E)** $\sqrt{2\pi}$

Answer (D): The area of a unit circle is $\pi \times 1^2 = \pi$. Since the area of the square is π, it must have a side length of $\sqrt{\pi}$.

6. 5 bops is equal to 20 gops and 3 gops is equal to 7 dops. How many bops is equal to 56 dops?

(A) 3 **(B)** 4 **(C)** 5 **(D)** 6 **(E)** 8

Answer (D): 7 dops is equal to 3 gops. So, $56 = 7 \times 8$ dops is equal to $24 = 3 \times 8$ gops. Since 5 bops is equal to 20 gops, 1 bop is equal to 4 gops and 24 gops is equal to 6 bops.

7. In a geometric sequence, the second term is 3 and the seventh term is 96. What is the fifth term of this sequence?

(A) 12   **(B)** 18   **(C)** 24   **(D)** 30   **(E)** 36

Answer (C): Let r be the common ratio of the geometric sequence. The 2nd term is 3; so after 5 terms, the 7th term must be $3r^5 = 96$. Therefore, the common ratio r is 2. The 5th term is 3 terms after the 2nd term, so it is $3 \times r^3 = 3 \times 2^3 = 24$.

8. How many 4-digit numbers are divisible by 5 and only contain even digits?

(A) 100   **(B)** 120   **(C)** 125   **(D)** 150   **(E)** 200

Answer (A): A number is divisible by 5 if it ends in 0 or 5. Since it contains only even digits, it must end in 0. The tens and hundreds digits each have 5 options: 0, 2, 4, 6, and 8. The thousands digit has 4 options: 2, 4, 6, and 8. By multiplication principle, there are $4 \times 5 \times 5 \times 1 = 100$ such numbers.

9. When an upward escalator is not working Alice can walk down in half a minute, using 60 steps. When she stands at the top and the escalator is moving she counts 75 steps of the escalator going by every minute. How many seconds will it take Alice to walk down the moving escalator?

(A) 45   **(B)** 60   **(C)** 75   **(D)** 80   **(E)** 90

Answer (D): Alice walks 60 steps in half a minute, so she walks at a rate of 120 steps per minute. When Alice walks down the moving escalator, the escalators brings Alice up 75 steps per minute. Thus she would have a net downwards motion of $120 - 75 = 45$ steps per minute. This rate is the same as 15 steps in 20 seconds or 60 steps in 80 seconds.

10. In a bag, there are six marbles: four red and two green. Bob starts randomly drawing marbles from the bag one at a time without replacement. What is the probability that the third marble he draws is green?

    (A) $\dfrac{1}{6}$ **(B)** $\dfrac{1}{3}$ **(C)** $\dfrac{1}{2}$ **(D)** $\dfrac{2}{3}$ **(E)** $\dfrac{5}{6}$

    Answer (B): We can represent Bob's drawing order by rearranging all the marbles from left to right in a line. We would like to find the probability that the third marble in the line is green. The third marble can be any of the 6 marbles, each being equally likely and only 2 of those possibilities are green. Hence, the answer is $\dfrac{2}{6} = \dfrac{1}{3}$.

11. How many of the elements in $\{-2020, -2019, \ldots, 2019, 2020\}$ are perfect squares?

    (A) 44   **(B)** 45   **(C)** 88   **(D)** 89   **(E)** 90

    Answer (B): Since $44^2 < 2020 < 45^2$, the perfect squares in the set are $0^2, 1^2, \ldots, 44^2$. There are $1 + 44 = 45$ of them.

12. What is the largest divisor of 210 that has no prime factor larger than 6?

    (A) 30   **(B)** 45   **(C)** 60   **(D)** 105   **(E)** 210

    Answer (A): We are looking for a factor of $210 = 2 \times 3 \times 5 \times 7$ that is not a multiple of 7. Counting in all the primes except for 7, we get $2 \times 3 \times 5 = 30$.

13. At Alpha Middle School, 60% of the students like swimming and 40% of the students like dancing. Among the students who like swimming, 20% like dancing. What percent of the people who like dancing do not like swimming?

    (A) 30%   **(B)** 40%   **(C)** 50%   **(D)** 60%   **(E)** 70%

    Answer (E): Since 20% or one fifth of the students who like swimming also like dancing, we see that $\dfrac{1}{5} \times 60\% = 12\%$ of the students like both swimming and dancing. This leaves us with $40\% - 12\% = 28\%$ of the students who like dancing but not swimming which is $\dfrac{28\%}{40\%} = 70\%$ of the students who like dancing.

14. A triangle has side lengths 8, 15, and 17. What is the length of the shortest altitude of the triangle?

    (A) $\dfrac{60}{17}$ (B) $\dfrac{35}{8}$ (C) $\dfrac{120}{17}$ (D) 8   (E) $\dfrac{35}{4}$

    Answer (C): The area of a triangle is half the base times height, so the product of side length and corresponding height is the same for all three sides. Thus the shortest altitude corresponds to the longest side, which has length 17. Because $8^2 + 15^2 = 17^2$, the triangle is a right triangle, with legs 8 and 15 and area $\dfrac{8 \times 15}{2} = 60$. If h is the shortest height, then using $\dfrac{1}{17 \times h} = 60$ we find that $h = \dfrac{120}{17}$.

15. How many ordered triples (x, y, z) of distinct integers are there satisfying

    $$(x - y)z = 4\left(\frac{1}{x} - \frac{1}{y}\right)?$$

    (A) 12   (B) 18   (C) 21   (D) 24   (E) 48

    Answer (A): Note that the right hand side simplifies to $4\left(\dfrac{y - x}{xy}\right)$. Since $x \neq y$, we can divide both sides of the equation by $x - y \neq 0$ to get $z = -\dfrac{4}{xy}$ or $xyz = -4$. Solutions with distinct integers are permutations of $(1, 2, -2)$ and $(1, -1, 4)$. Each has $3! = 6$ permutations; so there are 12 solutions.

16. The bottom of a pendulum, instead of swinging side to side, moves in a circular path while the string traces out the lateral face of a cone. If the length of the string holding the pendulum is 13 meters, and the length of one circular path is 10π meters, what is the volume of this cone, in cubic meters?

    (A) 50π (B) 75π (C) 100π (D) 120π (E) 150π

16

Answer (C): The slant height of this cone is 13. The circumference of this cone is 10π, so the radius must be 5. This means that the height of the cone is $\sqrt{13^2 - 5^2} = 12$. Since the volume of a cone is $\frac{1}{3}\pi r^2 h$, the volume of this cone is $\dfrac{\pi \times 5^2 \times 12}{3} = 100\pi$.

17. Two real numbers satisfy the following properties:

    (a) when they are both increased by 5, their product doubles, and
    (b) when they are both decreased by 3, their product halves.

    What is the product when the two real numbers are both increased by 2?

    (A) 300   **(B)** 330   **(C)** 360   **(D)** 390   **(E)** 420

    Answer (B): Let the two real numbers be a and b. We have

    $$(a+5)(b+5) = 2ab \text{ and } (a-3)(b-3) = \frac{ab}{2}.$$

    Expanding and rewriting, we get

    $$ab - 5a - 5b = 25 \text{ and } ab - 6a - 6b = -18.$$

    Subtracting the two equations gives $a + b = 43$. Substituting this value in either equation then gives $ab = 240$. Finally,

    $$(a+2)(b+2) = ab + 2(a+b) + 4 = 240 + 2 \times 43 + 4 = 330.$$

18. A round table has five chairs labeled 1 through 5. How many ways are there for three girls and two boys to sit around the table, if the two boys may not sit next to each other?

    (A) 5   **(B)** 10   **(C)** 12   **(D)** 30   **(E)** 60

    Answer (E): If the boys do not sit together, they must sit with one seat between them, giving 5 ways to choose the two seats. There are $2! = 2$ permutations for the boys and $3! = 6$ permutation for the girls, so the total number of seatings is $5 \cdot 2 \cdot 6 = 60$.

Alternatively, after one of the boys sit wherever he wants, there are 4 seats left and the other boy can only sit in 2 of them. Thus the chance of two boys not sitting next to each other is $1/2$. This means only half of all the sitting arrangements work. So the answer is $\dfrac{5!}{2} = 60$.

19. Out of the regular polygons with at most 100 sides, how many have interior angles that are integers when measured in degrees?

(A) 18   (B) 19   (C) 20   (D) 21   (E) 22

Answer (B): The interior and exterior angles are supplementary angles (summing to 180 degrees). Hence (in degrees) the interior angle is an integer if and only if the exterior angle is an integer. The degree measure of an exterior angle of a regular n-gon is $\dfrac{360}{n}$. For this to be an integer, n must be a factor of 360 which has prime factorization $2^3 \times 3^2 \times 5$. This means there are $(3+1)(2+1)(1+1) = 24$ factors. However, we cannot count factors where $n < 3$ or $n > 100$ (namely 1, 2, 120, 180, and 360), as they do not form a polygon with at most 100 sides. Subtracting these 5 cases, we end up with $24 - 5 = 19$ such polygons.

20. In the diagram below, each of the four unit circles is tangent to two other circles, and the diagram is identical after a 90 degree rotation around its center. What is the area of the shaded region?

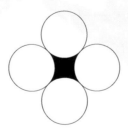

(A) $1 - \dfrac{\pi}{4}$ (B) $2 - \dfrac{\pi}{2}$ (C) $\dfrac{3}{4}$ (D) $\dfrac{\pi}{4}$ (E) $4 - \pi$

Answer (E): If we connect the centers of the four squares as shown, we create a square with side length $1 + 1 = 2$. (This figure must be a square because of the rotational symmetry given in the problem.)

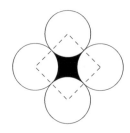

Note that the shaded area is the area of the square minus the areas of four quarter unit circles (or a full unit circle). This gives the answer $2^2 - \pi \times 1^2 = 4 - \pi$.

21. What is the probability that a randomly chosen positive factor of 60^{60} is odd?

(A) $\dfrac{1}{121}$ (B) $\dfrac{1}{120}$ (C) $\dfrac{1}{61}$ (D) $\dfrac{1}{60}$ (E) $\dfrac{1}{2}$

Answer (A): $60^{60} = (2^2 \times 3 \times 5)^{60} = 2^{120} \times 3^{60} \times 5^{60}$. Any factor must be of the form $2^a \times 3^b \times 5^c$ where $0 \le a \le 120$, $0 \le b \le 60$, and $0 \le c \le 60$. a, b, c are random and independent of each other. For the number to be odd, it must have 0 factors of 2, which gives only one working possibility for a over a total of 121 possibilities. Therefore, the answer is $\dfrac{1}{121}$.

22. What is the remainder when 2^{8888} is divided by 18?

(A) 2   (B) 4   (C) 8   (D) 10   (E) 14

Answer (B): Looking at small numbers we see that the remainders of

$$2^1, 2^2, 2^3, 2^4, 2^5, 2^6, 2^7, 2^8, \ldots$$

when divided by 18 are

$$2, 4, 8, 16, 14, 10, 2, 4, \ldots$$

This sequence repeats itself every 6 terms which means repeatedly subtracting 6 from the exponent of 2^{8888} does not change its remainder. Since 8888 is 2 more than a multiple of 6, we conclude that 2^{8888} has the same remainder as $2^2 = 4$.

23. Random Richard constructs a right triangle with two legs with length each chosen uniformly at random from the interval $(0, 2)$. To the nearest hundredth, what is the probability that the hypotenuse of Richard's triangle is greater than 2?

(A) 0.21   **(B)** 0.23   **(C)** 0.25   **(D)** 0.27   **(E)** 0.29

Answer (A): If we let one of the legs have length x and the other leg have length y, then the hypotenuse has length $\sqrt{x^2 + y^2}$. We can convert this problem to a 2D grid: if we look at the square made from $\{0 \leq x \leq 2, 0 \leq y \leq 2\}$, then the question is asking us the probability that a random point in that square satisfies the inequality $\sqrt{x^2 + y^2} > 2$, or $x^2 + y^2 > 4$. The equality $x^2 + y^2 = 4$ corresponds to a quarter-circle in the square, so the inequality $x^2 + y^2 > 4$ corresponds to the area of the region outside of the quarter circle (distance to origin is greater than 2). The quarter circle has radius 2, so its area is π. The entire square has area 4, so the area of the region outside of the quarter circle but inside the square is $4 - \pi$. This means the probability a random point inside the square is outside of the quarter circle is $\frac{4-\pi}{4} \approx 0.21$.

24. Justin has a whiteboard with the integers from 5 to 20 written:

$$5, 6, 7, \ldots, 20.$$

Every minute, he chooses two of the numbers a and b on the board, erases them and writes $a + b - 10$ instead. He stops when there is only one number on the board. To his surprise, after trying this process many times, he always ends up with the same number. What is this number?

(A) 25   **(B)** 50   **(C)** 100   **(D)** 150   **(E)** 200

Answer (B): Consider how the sum of the numbers change over time. Note that at each step, the number of numbers on the board decreases by 1 and the sum of the numbers on the board decreases by $(a + b) - (a + b - 10) = 10$. At the beginning, there are 16 numbers on the board so it would take 15 steps to reduce them to a single number. The initial sum is $5 + 6 + \ldots + 20 = 16 \times \left(\dfrac{5 + 20}{2}\right) = 200$. After 15 steps, the sum would reduce to $200 - 15 \times 10 = 50$. Since there is only one number left at this point with a sum of 50, that number itself must be 50.

Alternatively, Justin can start with the pairs $(5, 20)$, $(6, 19)$, etc. Each pair has a sum of 25 so he replaces them with 15. After these steps, he would be left with eight 15's.

Next, choosing four $(15, 15)$ pairs and replacing them with $15 + 15 - 10 = 20$'s, he would be left with four 20's. Proceeding similarly, he would next have two 30's and finally a single $30 + 30 - 10 = 50$ left.

25. In trapezoid $ABCD$, $AB \parallel CD$, $AB = 1$, and $CD = 3$. Lines $\overline{DA}$ and $\overline{CB}$ intersect at point P, and the area of triangle PDB is 6. What is the area of trapezoid $ABCD$?

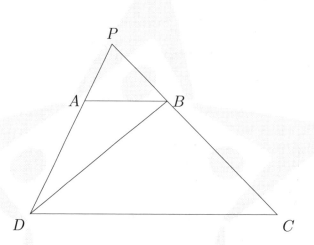

(A) 12   **(B)** 14   **(C)** 15   **(D)** 16   **(E)** 18

Answer (D): We want to compute the area of $ABCD$, but since we are given point P, we should first use the fact that $\triangle PAB \sim \triangle PDC$. If we denote the area of PAB as x, then the area of PDC must be $9x$, as the corresponding side length ratio of $AB : DC$ is 1:3. This means the area of $ABCD$ equals $9x - x = 8x$. Now, we want to express the area of PDB in terms of x in order to compute x.

We see that triangles ABD and BCD have bases of length 1 and 3 but share the same height, so their areas are in a ratio of 1:3. Since the sum of their areas is the area of $ABCD$, or $8x$, the two areas must be $2x$ and $6x$, respectively. This means that the area of PBD can be expressed as $x + 2x = 3x$. The problem tells us $3x = 6$, so $x = 2$ and the area of $ABCD$ is $8x = 16$.

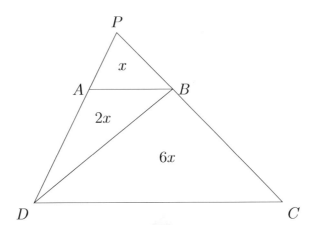

AMC 8 PRACTICE TESTS VOL 1

TEST-2

INSTRUCTIONS

1. This is a twenty-five question multiple choice test. Each question is followed by answers marked A, B, C, D and E. Only one of these is correct.

2. There is no penalty for guessing. Your score is the number of correct answers.

3. Only scratch paper, graph paper, rulers, protractors, and erasers are allowed as aids. Calculators are NOT allowed. No problems on the test *require* the use of a calculator.

4. Figures are not necessarily drawn to scale.

5. You will have **40 minutes** to complete the test.

24

1. Evaluate $1 + \cfrac{1 + \cfrac{1+1}{\frac{1}{\frac{1}{1}}}}{1 + \cfrac{1}{1+1}}$.

    (A) 3   (B) 4   (C) 5   (D) 6   (E) 7

2. Alvin is filling up his 60 gallon bathtub, but forgets to plug the drain. If water flows in at 5 gallons per minute and simultaneously leaves the drain at 3 gallons per minute, how many minutes will it take to fill up the bathtub?

    (A) 12   (B) 16   (C) 20   (D) 24   (E) 30

3. What is 25% of 125% of 80?

    (A) 10   (B) 20   (C) 25   (D) 30   (E) 50

4. Will has two boxes: Box A contains 1 red ball and 2 blue balls. Box B contains 2 red balls and 1 blue ball. He chooses one of the boxes at random and then randomly takes a ball from that box. What is the probability that the ball is red?

    (A) $\dfrac{1}{6}$ (B) $\dfrac{1}{3}$ (C) $\dfrac{1}{2}$ (D) $\dfrac{2}{3}$ (E) $\dfrac{5}{6}$

5. During a trip, Evan drives first at 30 mph for 40 minutes and then at 60 mph for 80 minutes. What is his average speed in mph?

    (A) 35 mph   (B) 40 mph   (C) 45 mph   (D) 50 mph   (E) 55 mph

6. A circle is inscribed in a square of area 40. What is the area of the circle?

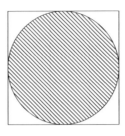

(A) $\sqrt{10}\,\pi$ (B) $2\sqrt{10}\,\pi$ (C) $4\sqrt{5}\,\pi$ (D) 10π (E) 40π

7. In Alpha Middle School, $\frac{2}{3}$ of the students like apples and $\frac{5}{6}$ of the students like oranges. What is the least possible percent of students who like both fruits?

(A) 10%   (B) 20%   (C) 30%   (D) 40%   (E) 50%

8. Alice, Bob, Charlie, and Dan are going to the movies. When they arrive, they find only four seats left, all in the same row next to each other. In how many ways can they sit so that Alice and Bob sit next to each other?

(A) 3   (B) 6   (C) 8   (D) 12   (E) 24

9. Yalini and Zillian both leave San Jose at the same time to go to Los Angeles. Yalini drives at a constant speed for the whole trip. Zillian drives at 50 mph for the first half of the distance and 30 mph for the rest. If they both arrive at the same time, what was Yalini's speed?

(A) 35 mph   (B) 37.5 mph   (C) 40 mph   (D) 42.5 mph   (E) 45 mph

10. Four numbers are chosen from the set $3, 6, 12, 27, 48$ so that the product is a perfect square. What is the number that was not chosen?

(A) 3   (B) 6   (C) 12   (D) 27   (E) 48

11. What is the units digit of $9^{8^{7^{\cdot^{\cdot^{\cdot^{2^1}}}}}}$?

(A) 1   (B) 3   (C) 5   (D) 7   (E) 9

12. What is the difference between the maximum and minimum number of regions that can be formed by two non-parallel lines and a triangle?

(A) 1   (B) 2   (C) 3   (D) 4   (E) 5

13. What is x if

$$\sqrt{x + \sqrt{x + \sqrt{x + \cdots}}} = 2?$$

(A) $\frac{1}{2}$ (B) 1   (C) $\sqrt{2}$ (D) 2   (E) $2\sqrt{2}$

14. Bill draws a regular hexagon. Jill measures the distance between the two opposite vertices of the hexagon as $2\sqrt{2}$. What is the area of the hexagon?

(A) $\sqrt{3}$ (B) $2\sqrt{3}$ (C) $3\sqrt{3}$ (D) $4\sqrt{3}$ (E) $5\sqrt{3}$

15. The sum of two positive real numbers is equal to twice the sum of their reciprocals. What is the product of the two numbers?

(A) $\frac{1}{4}$ (B) $\frac{1}{2}$ (C) 1   (D) 2   (E) 4

16. A five-pointed star is formed by extending the sides of a regular pentagon. What is the sum of the ten interior angles of the star?

(A) $1440°$ (B) $1500°$ (C) $1600°$ (D) $1620°$ (E) $1800°$

17. Bob starts at vertex A of square $ABCD$. Every minute, he moves to an adjacent vertex of the square, moving clockwise with probability $\frac{1}{3}$, and counterclockwise with probability $\frac{2}{3}$. After four minutes, what is the probability that he is at vertex A?

(A) $\dfrac{1}{3}$ **(B)** $\dfrac{40}{81}$ **(C)** $\dfrac{1}{2}$ **(D)** $\dfrac{41}{81}$ **(E)** $\dfrac{2}{3}$

18. How many real values x satisfy $\Big|\big||x-1|-1\big|-1\Big|=1$?

(A) 0   **(B)** 1   **(C)** 2   **(D)** 3   **(E)** 4

19. What are the last two digits of $7^{7^{7^7}}$?

(A) 01   **(B)** 07   **(C)** 43   **(D)** 49   **(E)** 77

20. Adam the Ant is going from his house located at $(0,0)$ to a restaurant located at $(4,4)$. At each step, Adam can move either one unit upwards or one unit to the right. However, Annie the Anteater lives at $(2,2)$. How many ways can Adam get to his destination without passing through Annie's house?

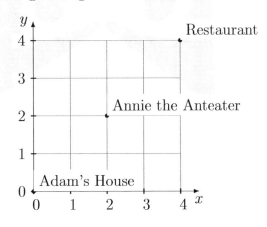

(A) 12   **(B)** 34   **(C)** 36   **(D)** 50   **(E)** 70

21. Isabelle has a kite (a quadrilateral with two pairs of adjacent equal-length sides) inscribed in a circle of radius 5. Given that one side of the kite has length 6, find the radius of another circle inscribed inside the kite.

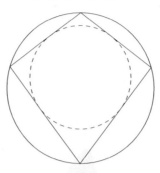

(A) $\dfrac{12}{5}$ (B) $\dfrac{5}{2}$ (C) $\dfrac{8}{3}$ (D) $\dfrac{24}{7}$ (E) $\dfrac{14}{3}$

22. In the figure below, $ABCDEF$ is a regular hexagon with side length 2. A circle is inscribed in the hexagon. Diagonal AC intersects the circle at points P and Q. Compute AP.

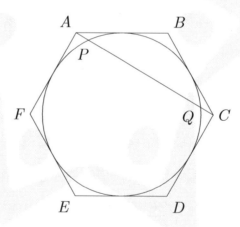

(A) $\dfrac{\sqrt{3}}{6}$ (B) $\sqrt{3} - \sqrt{2}$ (C) $\dfrac{1}{3}$ (D) $\sqrt{6} - 2$ (E) $2\sqrt{3} - 3$

23. The area and perimeter of a right triangle with integer side lengths are numerically equal. What is the sum of all possible areas of such triangles?

(A) 6   (B) 24   (C) 32   (D) 54   (E) 60

24. Flora's favorite positive number N has the following properties:
    (a) It is the product of two or more distinct odd primes.
    (b) If she subtracts 1 from each of the prime divisors of N and then multiplies, the product would be 60.
    What is the sum of all possible values of N?

    (A) 138   **(B)** 154   **(C)** 170   **(D)** 231   **(E)** 300

25. Three points are chosen on each side of a square, aside from the vertices of the square. Lines are drawn connecting every pair of the 12 points that are on different sides of the square. If no three lines concur at the same point inside the square, at how many points do two of the lines intersect inside the square?

    (A) 66   **(B)** 81   **(C)** 459   **(D)** 495   **(E)** 512

Test-2 Answer Key

1. A
2. E
3. C
4. C
5. D
6. D
7. E
8. D
9. B
10. B
11. A
12. C
13. D
14. C
15. D
16. A
17. D
18. E
19. C
20. B
21. D
22. B
23. D
24. C
25. C

Test-2 Solutions

1. Evaluate $1 + \dfrac{1 + \dfrac{1+1}{\frac{1}{1}}}{1 + \dfrac{1}{1+1}}$.

   (A) 3   (B) 4   (C) 5   (D) 6   (E) 7

   Answer (A): Simplifying, we get

   $$1 + \dfrac{1 + \dfrac{1+1}{\frac{1}{1}}}{1 + \dfrac{1}{1+1}} = 1 + \dfrac{1+2}{1+0.5} = 1 + \dfrac{3}{1.5} = 1 + 2 = 3.$$

2. Alvin is filling up his 60 gallon bathtub, but forgets to plug the drain. If water flows in at 5 gallons per minute and simultaneously leaves the drain at 3 gallons per minute, how many minutes will it take to fill up the bathtub?

   (A) 12   (B) 16   (C) 20   (D) 24   (E) 30

   Answer (E): In 1 minute, the level of water will increase by $5 - 3 = 2$ gallons. Thus, it will take $\frac{60}{2} = 30$ minutes to fill up the bathtub.

3. What is 25% of 125% of 80?

   (A) 10   (B) 20   (C) 25   (D) 30   (E) 50

   Answer (C): 125% of 80 is $\dfrac{5}{4} \times 80 = 100$, and 25% of 100 is 25.

4. Will has two boxes: Box A contains 1 red ball and 2 blue balls. Box B contains 2 red balls and 1 blue ball. He chooses one of the boxes at random and then randomly takes a ball from that box. What is the probability that the ball is red?

(A) $\frac{1}{6}$ (B) $\frac{1}{3}$ (C) $\frac{1}{2}$ (D) $\frac{2}{3}$ (E) $\frac{5}{6}$

Answer (C): Notice that the two boxes are symmetric regarding the number of red and blue balls. Thus,

$$P(\text{red}) = P(\text{blue}) = \frac{1}{2}.$$

Alternatively, computing the probability gives

$$\frac{1}{2} \times \frac{1}{3} + \frac{1}{2} \times \frac{2}{3} = \frac{1}{6} + \frac{2}{6} = \frac{1}{2}.$$

5. During a trip, Evan drives first at 30 mph for 40 minutes and then at 60 mph for 80 minutes. What is his average speed in mph?

(A) 35 mph   (B) 40 mph   (C) 45 mph   (D) 50 mph   (E) 55 mph

Answer (D): The two segments of the trip take 2/3 and 4/3 hours. Thus Evan drives a total distance of

$$30 \times \frac{2}{3} + 60 \times \frac{4}{3} = 100 \text{ miles.}$$

It takes him $40 + 80 = 120$ minutes or 2 hours. His average speed is $\frac{100}{2} = 50$ mph.

6. A circle is inscribed in a square of area 40. What is the area of the circle?

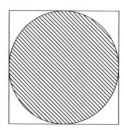

(A) $\sqrt{10}\,\pi$ **(B)** $2\sqrt{10}\,\pi$ **(C)** $4\sqrt{5}\,\pi$ **(D)** 10π **(E)** 40π

Answer (D): We can find that the side length of the square is $\sqrt{40} = 2\sqrt{10}$, so the radius of the circle is $\sqrt{10}$. Using the area formula, we find that the area of the circle is $\left(\sqrt{10}\right)^2 \pi = 10\pi$.

7. In Alpha Middle School, $\frac{2}{3}$ of the students like apples and $\frac{5}{6}$ of the students like oranges. What is the least possible percent of students who like both fruits?

(A) 10%   **(B)** 20%   **(C)** 30%   **(D)** 40%   **(E)** 50%

Answer (E): Only $\frac{1}{6}$ of the students do not like oranges. Even if all of these students like apples, among the remaining $\frac{5}{6}$ of the students who like oranges, there must be an additional $\frac{2}{3} - \frac{1}{6} = \frac{1}{2}$ who like apples. Thus, at least 50% of the students like both fruits.

8. Alice, Bob, Charlie, and Dan are going to the movies. When they arrive, they find only four seats left, all in the same row next to each other. In how many ways can they sit so that Alice and Bob sit next to each other?

(A) 3   **(B)** 6   **(C)** 8   **(D)** 12   **(E)** 24

Answer (D): We first consider where Alice and Bob sit. Number the seats 1 to 4 from left to right. Then Alice and Bob can sit in seats 1 and 2, 2 and 3, or 3 and 4. Once they choose the two seats, they have 2 choices: with Alice on the left and Bob on the right, or with Alice on the right and Bob on the left. After Alice and Bob choose their seats, Charlie and Dan have two seats left, and they also have 2 ways to choose their seats. Therefore, the group has $3 \times 2 \times 2 = 12$ ways to sit.

Alternatively, considering Alice and Bob as one group, we need to order three people or groups: Alice & Bob, Charlie, and Dan. This can be done in $3! = 6$ ways. Alice and Bob can choose their seats in 2 ways. This gives us $6 \times 2 = 12$ ways.

3636

9. Yalini and Zillian both leave San Jose at the same time to go to Los Angeles. Yalini drives at a constant speed for the whole trip. Zillian drives at 50 mph for the first half of the distance and 30 mph for the rest. If they both arrive at the same time, what was Yalini's speed?

(A) 35 mph **(B)** 37.5 mph **(C)** 40 mph **(D)** 42.5 mph **(E)** 45 mph

Answer (B): Let's say the total trip is $300k$ miles. It takes Zillian $\dfrac{150k}{50} + \dfrac{150k}{30} = 3k + 5k = 8k$ hours. Hence, it takes $8k$ hours for Yalini as well and her average speed is $\dfrac{300k}{8k} = 37.5$ mph.

10. Four numbers are chosen from the set $3, 6, 12, 27, 48$ so that the product is a perfect square. What is the number that was not chosen?

(A) 3 **(B)** 6 **(C)** 12 **(D)** 27 **(E)** 48

Answer (B): Observe that $3 \times 27 = 9^2$ and $12 \times 48 = 24^2$ are both squares. Hence, their product is also a perfect square and the fifth number must be 6. To see that 6 is the only answer, note that the product of all of the numbers is $2^7 \times 3^7$. We want to divide this by one of the numbers and get the product of the remaining four numbers to be a perfect square. To have both powers of 2 and 3 even, we need to divide this by 2 to an odd power multiplied by 3 to an odd power. The only such number among the five numbers is $6 = 2^1 \times 3^1$.

11. What is the units digit of $9^{8^{7^{\cdot^{\cdot^{2^1}}}}}$?

(A) 1 **(B)** 3 **(C)** 5 **(D)** 7 **(E)** 9

Answer (A): We experiment by listing out the powers of 9: $9^1 = 9$, $9^2 = 81$, $9^3 = 729$, etc. We notice that the units digit of 9^n is 9 when n is odd and 1 when n is even, so because the exponent here is even, the answer is 1.

12. What is the difference between the maximum and minimum number of regions that can be formed by two non-parallel lines and a triangle?

(A) 1   **(B)** 2   **(C)** 3   **(D)** 4   **(E)** 5

Answer (C): Since the two lines are not parallel they intersect at a point, and divide the plane into 4 regions. The triangle can further add at least 1 to the number regions, if it is entirely contained in one of the 4 regions, and at most 4 to the number of regions, if it has parts in each of the 4 regions. Hence, the difference is $(4 + 4) - (4 + 1) = 3$.

13. What is x if
$$\sqrt{x + \sqrt{x + \sqrt{x + \cdots}}} = 2?$$

(A) $\dfrac{1}{2}$ **(B)** 1   **(C)** $\sqrt{2}$ **(D)** 2   **(E)** $2\sqrt{2}$

Answer (D): Substituting
$$\sqrt{x + \sqrt{x + \sqrt{x + \cdots}}} = 2$$

inside the first square root, we get
$$\sqrt{x + 2} = 2.$$

Squaring both sides we get $x + 2 = 4$ and $x = 2$.

Note that in general, if
$$\sqrt{x + \sqrt{x + \sqrt{x + \cdots}}} = n$$
for some positive number n, we can similarly get $\sqrt{x + n} = n$, which gives $x = n^2 - n$.

14. Bill draws a regular hexagon. Jill measures the distance between the two opposite vertices of the hexagon as $2\sqrt{2}$. What is the area of the hexagon?

(A) $\sqrt{3}$ **(B)** $2\sqrt{3}$ **(C)** $3\sqrt{3}$ **(D)** $4\sqrt{3}$ **(E)** $5\sqrt{3}$

Answer (C): The longest diagonal in a hexagon is equal to twice its side length.

Using this information, the hexagon's side length is $\sqrt{2}$. Since a hexagon can be split into six equilateral triangles, we only need to compute the area of one of these. The area of a equilateral triangle with side length s is $\dfrac{s^2\sqrt{3}}{4}$. Plugging in $s = \sqrt{2}$, we get that the area of 1 triangle is $\dfrac{\sqrt{3}}{2}$. Since we have six triangles, the answer is $6 \times \dfrac{\sqrt{3}}{2} = 3\sqrt{3}$.

15. The sum of two positive real numbers is equal to twice the sum of their reciprocals. What is the product of the two numbers?

(A) $\dfrac{1}{4}$ (B) $\dfrac{1}{2}$ (C) 1   (D) 2   (E) 4

Answer (D): Let a and b be the two numbers. We are given that

$$a + b = 2\left(\frac{1}{a} + \frac{1}{b}\right).$$

Then we get

$$a + b = 2\left(\frac{a+b}{ab}\right)$$

Canceling the $a + b$ terms, which cannot be 0 since a and b are positive, reduces this to $1 = \dfrac{2}{ab}$ and we conclude that $ab = 2$.

16. A five-pointed star is formed by extending the sides of a regular pentagon. What is the sum of the ten interior angles of the star?

(A) $1440°$ (B) $1500°$ (C) $1600°$ (D) $1620°$ (E) $1800°$

Answer (A): Note that we can decompose the star into 8 triangles: 3 inside the pentagon, and 5 outside. The sum of the interior angles of the star is the same as the sum of the angles of these 8 triangles combined. The sum of the angles of a triangle is $180°$. Hence, the answer is $8 \times 180° = 1440°$.

17. Bob starts at vertex A of square $ABCD$. Every minute, he moves to an adjacent vertex of the square, moving clockwise with probability $\frac{1}{3}$, and counterclockwise with

probability $\frac{2}{3}$. After four minutes, what is the probability that he is at vertex A?

(A) $\dfrac{1}{3}$ (B) $\dfrac{40}{81}$ (C) $\dfrac{1}{2}$ (D) $\dfrac{41}{81}$ (E) $\dfrac{2}{3}$

Answer (D): Note that after any even number of minutes, Bob must be at either A or C. Thus, we can reduce the problem to two vertices, A and C. After two minutes, the probability of switching from one vertex to the other is

$$\left(\frac{1}{3}\right)^2 + \left(\frac{2}{3}\right)^2 = \frac{5}{9}$$

and the probability of staying at the same vertex is

$$2 \times \frac{1}{3} \times \frac{2}{3} = \frac{4}{9}.$$

Thus, the probability of being at vertex A after 4 minutes is

$$\left(\frac{5}{9}\right)^2 + \left(\frac{4}{9}\right)^2 = \frac{41}{81}.$$

18. How many real values x satisfy $\left|\,\big|\,|x-1|-1\big|-1\right| = 1$?

(A) 0   (B) 1   (C) 2   (D) 3   (E) 4

Answer (E): Starting from the outside and working inwards, we get the following:

$$
\begin{aligned}
\big|\,|x-1|-1\big|-1 &= \pm 1 \\
\big|\,|x-1|-1\big| &= 1 \pm 1 = 0, 2 \\
|x-1|-1 &= 0, \pm 2 \\
|x-1| &= 1 \pm 0, 1 \pm 2 = \pm 1, 3 \\
x-1 &= \pm 1, \pm 3 \\
x &= 1 \pm 1, 1 \pm 3.
\end{aligned}
$$

Thus, we have 4 solutions: $-2, 0, 2, 4$.

19. What are the last two digits of $7^{7^{7^7}}$?

(A) 01   (B) 07   (C) 43   (D) 49   (E) 77

Answer (C): Listing the last two digits of small powers of 7, we find that

$$7^1, 7^2, 7^3, 7^4, \cdots$$

end in

$$7, 49, 43, 01, \cdots$$

the pattern repeating itself every four numbers. Let $n = 7^{7^7}$. To find the last two digits of 7^n, we need to find the remainder of n when divided by 4. The remainders of powers of 7 when divided by 4 follow a pattern of

$$3, 1, 3, 1, \cdots$$

with odd powers giving remainder 3 and even powers giving remainder 1. Since 7^7 is odd, $n = 7^{7^7}$ has remainder 3 when divided by 4. We conclude that the last two digits of 7^n are the same as the last two digits of 7^3, or 43.

20. Adam the Ant is going from his house located at $(0,0)$ to a restaurant located at $(4,4)$. At each step, Adam can move either one unit upwards or one unit to the right. However, Annie the Anteater lives at $(2,2)$. How many ways can Adam get to his destination without passing through Annie's house?

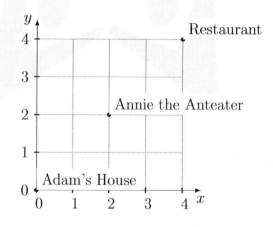

(A) 12   (B) 34   (C) 36   (D) 50   (E) 70

Answer (B): We will use complementary counting. Each of Adam's paths can be thought as a series of 4 up arrows ($\uparrow$) and 4 right arrows ($\rightarrow$), arranged in a line. This gives $\binom{4+4}{4} = \binom{8}{4} = 70$ paths total. Every path that goes through Annie's house can be seen as a path from $(0,0)$ to $(2,2)$ followed by a path from $(2,2)$ to $(4,4)$. We find that there are $\binom{2+2}{2}^2 = \binom{4}{2}^2 = 6^2 = 36$ undesired paths. Therefore, the answer is $70 - 36 = 34$.

21. Isabelle has a kite (a quadrilateral with two pairs of adjacent equal-length sides) inscribed in a circle of radius 5. Given that one side of the kite has length 6, find the radius of another circle inscribed inside the kite.

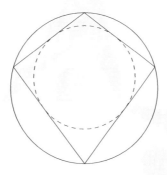

(A) $\dfrac{12}{5}$ (B) $\dfrac{5}{2}$ (C) $\dfrac{8}{3}$ (D) $\dfrac{24}{7}$ (E) $\dfrac{14}{3}$

Answer (D): Since the kite is inscribed in a circle, the diagonal of the kite that coincides with the line of symmetry is also the diameter of the big circle. This diagonal has length 10 and splits the kite into two right triangles. Since we are given that one of the legs has length 6, by the Pythagorean theorem, we find that the other leg must have length 8. If we connect the center of the small circle to the four vertices of the kite, they split the kite into four triangles. They all have a common height of r, the radius of the small circle, and bases of lengths 6, 6, 8, and 8. Hence, their areas sum to $\dfrac{6r}{2} + \dfrac{6r}{2} + \dfrac{8r}{2} + \dfrac{8r}{2} = 14r$ which is the total area of the kite. We can compute this another way by putting the two right triangles with legs 6 and 8, and get $\dfrac{6 \times 8}{2} \times 2 = 48$. Finally, equating these we get $14r = 48$ and $r = \dfrac{24}{7}$.

22. In the figure below, $ABCDEF$ is a regular hexagon with side length 2. A circle is inscribed in the hexagon. Diagonal AC intersects the circle at points P and Q. Compute AP.

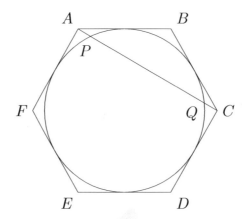

(A) $\dfrac{\sqrt{3}}{6}$ (B) $\sqrt{3}-\sqrt{2}$ (C) $\dfrac{1}{3}$ (D) $\sqrt{6}-2$ (E) $2\sqrt{3}-3$

Answer (B): Let the center of the hexagon be point O. Triangle AOB is an equilateral triangle of side length 2. Let point M be the intersection of lines AC and OB. To find AP we will compute $AM - PM$. Since triangles AOB and BOC are both equilateral, $ABCO$ is a rhombus. The diagonals of a rhombus bisect each other, so $OM = \dfrac{OB}{2} = 1$. OP is the radius of the circle, which is just the height of an equilateral triangle of side length 2, or $\sqrt{3}$. Now we have enough information to find AM and PM. Note that AM is also the height of equilateral triangle AOB, so $AM = \sqrt{3}$. Using the Pythagorean Theorem on triangle POM gives us $PM = \sqrt{(\sqrt{3})^2 - 1^2} = \sqrt{2}$. We conclude that $AP = \sqrt{3} - \sqrt{2}$.

23. The area and perimeter of a right triangle with integer side lengths are numerically equal. What is the sum of all possible areas of such triangles?

(A) 6   (B) 24   (C) 32   (D) 54   (E) 60

Answer (D): Let a, b, and c be the lengths of the two legs and the hypothenuse of the triangle. Since the area is numerically equal to the perimeter, we have

$$a + b + c = \frac{ab}{2}.$$

Rewriting this as

$$2c = ab - 2a - 2b$$

and squaring both sides, we get

$$4c^2 = (ab)^2 + 4a^2 + 4b^2 - 4a^2b - 4ab^2 + 8ab.$$

Using $c^2 = a^2 + b^2$ by Pythagorean Theorem reduces this to

$$0 = (ab)^2 - 4a^2b - 4ab^2 + 8ab$$

Dividing both sides by ab we get

$$0 = ab - 4a - 4b + 8.$$

We can use Simon's Favorite Factoring Trick by adding 8 to both sides and factoring to obtain

$$8 = (a-4)(b-4).$$

Therefore $\{a-4, b-4\} = \{1, 8\}$ or $\{2, 4\}$, so $\{a, b\} = \{5, 12\}$ or $\{6, 8\}$. These give us areas of $\dfrac{5 \times 12}{2} = 30$ and $\dfrac{6 \times 8}{2} = 24$, for a sum of 54.

24. Flora's favorite positive number N has the following properties:

    (a) It is the product of two or more distinct odd primes.
    (b) If she subtracts 1 from each of the prime divisors of N and then multiplies, the product would be 60.

What is the sum of all possible values of N?

(A) 138   **(B)** 154   **(C)** 170   **(D)** 231   **(E)** 300

Answer (C): Since N is odd, all of its prime divisors are odd and subtracting 1 gives even numbers with a product of 60. We can write 60 as a product of even numbers in only two ways: 2×30 and 6×10. These give N values $3 \times 31 = 93$ and $7 \times 11 = 77$, so the answer is $93 + 77 = 170$.

25. Three points are chosen on each side of a square, aside from the vertices of the square. Lines are drawn connecting every pair of the 12 points that are on different sides of the square. If no three lines concur at the same point inside the square, at how many points do two of the lines intersect inside the square?

(A) 66   **(B)** 81   **(C)** 459   **(D)** 495   **(E)** 512

Answer (C): Every time two lines intersect inside the square, by considering the four points on the two lines, we get a quadrilateral. Also for each quadrilateral with vertices among the 12 points, by joining the diagonals, we get an intersection point

44

inside the square, as long as the quadrilateral does not have three vertices on the same side of the square. Hence, the number of intersection points inside the square is the same as the number of such quadrilaterals.

There are

$$\binom{12}{4} = \frac{12 \times 11 \times 10 \times 9}{4!} = 495$$

ways to pick four points among the 12 points. However, $9 \times 4 = 36$ of these correspond to 3 of the points being on the same side, hence not giving an intersection point inside. The remaining 459 quadrilaterals give unique intersection points inside the square.

AMC 8 PRACTICE TESTS VOL 1

TEST-3

INSTRUCTIONS

1. This is a twenty-five question multiple choice test. Each question is followed by answers marked A, B, C, D and E. Only one of these is correct.

2. There is no penalty for guessing. Your score is the number of correct answers.

3. Only scratch paper, graph paper, rulers, protractors, and erasers are allowed as aids. Calculators are NOT allowed. No problems on the test *require* the use of a calculator.

4. Figures are not necessarily drawn to scale.

5. You will have **40 minutes** to complete the test.

1. A regular polygon has a perimeter of 100. If each side has length 5, how many sides does it have?

   (A) 5   (B) 10   (C) 20   (D) 25   (E) 100

2. What is the value of $\dfrac{2^3 + 1}{3^2 \times 1}$?

   (A) $\dfrac{7}{9}$ (B) $\dfrac{4}{5}$ (C) $\dfrac{8}{9}$ (D) $\dfrac{9}{10}$ (E) 1

3. Felix buys four pencils and three pens for $12. If a pen costs $2, what is the difference between the costs of a pencil and a pen, in cents?

   (A) 20   (B) 25   (C) 30   (D) 40   (E) 50

4. What is the fifteenth term of the arithmetic sequence $1, 4, 7, 10, \ldots$?

   (A) 37   (B) 40   (C) 43   (D) 46   (E) 49

5. If two raccoons can eat 20 watermelons in five minutes, how many watermelons can three raccoons eat in one minute?

   (A) 3   (B) 6   (C) 9   (D) 12   (E) 30

6. Evaluate the following: $(-5)^3 + (-4)^3 + (-3)^3 + \ldots + 6^3 + 7^3$.

   (A) 127   (B) 216   (C) 343   (D) 529   (E) 559

7. A bag contains 4 red marbles and 4 green marbles. We draw two marbles randomly without replacement. What is the probability that we get one green marble and one red marble?

   (A) $\dfrac{1}{4}$ (B) $\dfrac{3}{7}$ (C) $\dfrac{1}{2}$ (D) $\dfrac{15}{28}$ (E) $\dfrac{4}{7}$

8. A circle is circumscribed around a rectangle with side lengths 6 and 8. What is the area of the circle?

   (A) 16π **(B)** 20π **(C)** 24π **(D)** 25π **(E)** 30π

9. A book has n pages, numbered from 1 through n. A total of 99 digits are used to number the pages. What is n?

   (A) 50   **(B)** 52   **(C)** 54   **(D)** 56   **(E)** 58

10. What is the sum of the digits of the largest two-digit prime number with digits that add up to a prime number?

    (A) 5   **(B)** 7   **(C)** 11   **(D)** 13   **(E)** 17

11. Positive numbers a and b satisfy

    $$a^{70} = b^{30} = 2.$$

    If $(ab)^n = 4$, what is n?

    (A) 42   **(B)** 44   **(C)** 46   **(D)** 48   **(E)** 50

12. In a city with very predictable weather, the probability that it rains on any given day is $\frac{1}{5}$. In this city, what is the probability that it rains at least one day in three consecutive days?

    (A) $\dfrac{60}{125}$ **(B)** $\dfrac{61}{125}$ **(C)** $\dfrac{62}{125}$ **(D)** $\dfrac{63}{125}$ **(E)** $\dfrac{64}{125}$

13. There are 12 teams in a double-elimination tournament, where a team is eliminated when they lose two games. In each game, two teams play and one of them loses. The tournament continues until only one team is left. At most how many games will the tournament have?

    (A) 20   **(B)** 21   **(C)** 22   **(D)** 23   **(E)** 24

14. Ayla, Ciana, and Ellen are three siblings. The product of their ages is 192. What is the smallest possible value for the sum of their ages?

(A) 18   (B) 19   (C) 20   (D) 21   (E) 22

15. Let $\triangle ABC$ be an isosceles triangle with $AB = AC = 6$. P is a point on side BC such that $BP = 3PC$. X is a point on AB such that $\overline{PX} \parallel \overline{CA}$. Y is a point on AC such that $\overline{PY} \parallel \overline{BA}$. What is the perimeter of quadrilateral $AXPY$?

(A) 10   (B) 12   (C) 15   (D) 16   (E) 20

16. Cindy thinks of a positive integer, adds four to it, squares the result, and subtracts 25. For how many starting numbers would Cindy end up with a negative number?

(A) 0   (B) 1   (C) 5   (D) 9   (E) 12

17. Sebastian has a bag of eight marbles, five red, and three blue. Without looking, he chooses two marbles from the bag without replacement. What is the probability that at least one of the marbles is blue?

(A) $\dfrac{1}{3}$ (B) $\dfrac{5}{14}$ (C) $\dfrac{1}{2}$ (D) $\dfrac{9}{14}$ (E) $\dfrac{2}{3}$

18. A sphere of radius 17 is cut with a plane, leaving it with two pieces with a circular flat side. When one of these pieces is set on a table with the flat side down, it reaches a height of 25 from the table. What is the radius of the circular flat side?

(A) 12   (B) 13   (C) 14   (D) 15   (E) 16

19. For a positive integer n, let $f(n)$ denote the number of positive factors of n. If the the product
$$f(a) \times f(b) \times f(c)$$
is odd for some distinct positive integers a, b, and c, what is the minimum value of $a + b + c$?

(A) 6   **(B)** 8   **(C)** 10   **(D)** 12   **(E)** 14

20. How many real numbers x satisfy
$$\left|2 - |x - 2|\right| + |x + 3| = 5?$$

(A) 0   **(B)** 1   **(C)** 2   **(D)** 4   **(E)** 6

21. Hasan loves to draw circles on a board and count the number of regions formed. When he draws one circle he gets two regions; inside and outside of the circle. When he draws two circles, he gets at most four regions. When he draws five circles, at most how many regions will he get?

(A) 20   **(B)** 22   **(C)** 26   **(D)** 30   **(E)** 32

22. In the diagram below, $ABCD$ is a square with side length 4. A circle is inscribed in $ABCD$ and diagonal $\overline{BD}$ intersects the circle at P. What is the length of $\overline{PC}$?

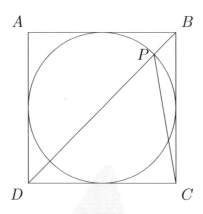

(A) $2\sqrt{3}$ (B) $\dfrac{7}{2}$ (C) $5 - \sqrt{2}$ (D) $2 + \sqrt{3}$ (E) $\sqrt{15}$

23. In the diagram below, $ABCD$ is a rectangle with $AB = 8$ and $BC = 6$. Points E and F are on $\overline{BD}$ such that $\overline{AE}$ and $\overline{CF}$ are perpendicular to $\overline{BD}$. What is the ratio of the area $AECF$ to the area of $ABCD$?

(A) $\dfrac{1}{4}$ (B) $\dfrac{7}{25}$ (C) $\dfrac{7}{24}$ (D) $\dfrac{17}{48}$ (E) $\dfrac{13}{24}$

24. Benjamin finds that a polynomial with degree four has leading coefficient 1 and roots 3, 5, 7, and 9. What is the sum of the coefficients of this polynomial?

(A) 0   (B) 24   (C) 206   (D) 384   (E) 945

25. Let N be the largest positive integer whose base-6 and base-11 representations are reverse of each other and neither representation ends in 0. What is the sum of the digits of N when it is written in base 10?

(A) 15   (B) 16   (C) 17   (D) 18   (E) 20

Test-3 Answer Key

1. C
2. E
3. E
4. C
5. B
6. E
7. E
8. D
9. C
10. E
11. A
12. B
13. D
14. A
15. B
16. A
17. D
18. D
19. E
20. C
21. B
22. A
23. B
24. D
25. B

Test-3 Solutions

1. A regular polygon has a perimeter of 100. If each side has length 5, how many sides does it have?

   (A) 5   (B) 10   (C) 20   (D) 25   (E) 100

   Answer (C): If there are n sides, then $5n = 100$ and $n = 20$.

2. What is the value of $\dfrac{2^3 + 1}{3^2 \times 1}$?

   (A) $\dfrac{7}{9}$ (B) $\dfrac{4}{5}$ (C) $\dfrac{8}{9}$ (D) $\dfrac{9}{10}$ (E) 1

   Answer (E): Evaluating the numerator and denominator, we get

   $$\frac{2^3 + 1}{3^2 \times 1} = \frac{8 + 1}{9 \times 1} = \frac{9}{9} = 1.$$

3. Felix buys four pencils and three pens for \$12. If a pen costs \$2, what is the difference between the costs of a pencil and a pen, in cents?

   (A) 20   (B) 25   (C) 30   (D) 40   (E) 50

   Answer (E): Four pencils and three pens cost \$12. Three pens cost $3 \times \$2 = \$6$. Hence, the remaining 4 pencils cost $\$12 - \$6 = \$6$ and each pencil costs \$1.50. The desired difference is $200 - 150 = 50$ cents.

4. What is the fifteenth term of the arithmetic sequence $1, 4, 7, 10, \ldots$?

(A) 37   (B) 40   (C) 43   (D) 46   (E) 49

Answer (C): We may express the kth term as $3k - 2$, so the 15th term is $3 \times 15 - 2 = 43$. Alternatively, this is an arithmetic sequence with first term 1 and common difference 3, so the fifteenth term is $1 + 3 \times (15 - 1) = 43$.

5. If two raccoons can eat 20 watermelons in five minutes, how many watermelons can three raccoons eat in one minute?

(A) 3   (B) 6   (C) 9   (D) 12   (E) 30

Answer (B): If two raccoons can eat 20 watermelons in 5 minutes, then 1 raccoon can eat half as many or 10 watermelons in the same amount of time. Thus, 1 raccoon eats 2 watermelons every minute. With three raccoons, this amounts to 6 watermelons.

6. Evaluate the following: $(-5)^3 + (-4)^3 + (-3)^3 + \ldots + 6^3 + 7^3$.

(A) 127   (B) 216   (C) 343   (D) 529   (E) 559

Answer (E): Since $(-x)^3 + x^3 = -x^3 + x^3 = 0$, we may cancel out $(-5)^3$ and 5^3, $(-4)^3$ and 4^3, etc. 0^3 evaluates to 0, so we are left with $6^3 + 7^3 = 216 + 343 = 559$.

7. A bag contains 4 red marbles and 4 green marbles. We draw two marbles randomly without replacement. What is the probability that we get one green marble and one red marble?

(A) $\dfrac{1}{4}$ (B) $\dfrac{3}{7}$ (C) $\dfrac{1}{2}$ (D) $\dfrac{15}{28}$ (E) $\dfrac{4}{7}$

Answer (E): We need to find the probability that the two marbles have different colors. We first pick one marble out of the bag. Regardless of its color, we want the next marble to be the opposite color. After picking one marble, there are 7 marbles left in the bag, 4 of which are of the opposite color. Therefore, the probability of the second marble having a different color than the first one is $\frac{4}{7}$.

8. A circle is circumscribed around a rectangle with side lengths 6 and 8. What is the area of the circle?

(A) 16π **(B)** 20π **(C)** 24π **(D)** 25π **(E)** 30π

Answer (D): The diagonal of the rectangle has length $\sqrt{6^2 + 8^2} = 10$. Since the diagonals of the rectangle coincide with diameters of the circle, the circle must have radius $\frac{10}{2} = 5$, and its area is $\pi(5)^2 = 25\pi$.

9. A book has n pages, numbered from 1 through n. A total of 99 digits are used to number the pages. What is n?

(A) 50 **(B)** 52 **(C)** 54 **(D)** 56 **(E)** 58

Answer (C): For pages 1 to 9, we use 1 digit per page, for a total of 9 digits. Thus we have $99 - 9 = 90$ digits left to number pages 10 through n. Each of these contains 2 digits, so there are $\frac{90}{2} = 45$ pages starting with 10. This means $n = 9 + 45 = 54$.

Alternatively, revising the numbering of the pages as $01, 02, 03, \ldots$ we are adding 9 more zeroes which brings the total number of digits used to 108. Now that each page uses exactly two digits, the number of pages is $n = \frac{108}{2} = 54$.

10. What is the sum of the digits of the largest two-digit prime number with digits that add up to a prime number?

(A) 5 **(B)** 7 **(C)** 11 **(D)** 13 **(E)** 17

Answer (E): Let $P = \overline{AB}$ be the two-digit prime number we are looking for. Since it is prime, B must be odd. The sum of its digits, $A + B$, is also prime. If this prime is 2, then $N = 11$. For any number larger, $A + B$ cannot be 2; so, it must be an odd prime. Since B is odd, A must be even. Looking at largest even and odd digits, we end up with the prime number $N = 89$ whose sum of digits is 17, which is indeed a prime number.

11. Positive numbers a and b satisfy

$$a^{70} = b^{30} = 2.$$

If $(ab)^n = 4$, what is n?

(A) 42   (B) 44   (C) 46   (D) 48   (E) 50

Answer (A): From the given equations we find that $a^{210} = 2^3$ and $b^{210} = 2^7$. Multiplying these gives
$$(ab)^{210} = 2^{10}.$$
Since $((ab)^{21})^{10} = 2^{10}$, we conclude that $(ab)^{21} = 2$. Squaring both sides gives $(ab)^{42} = 4$. So the answer is 42.

12. In a city with very predictable weather, the probability that it rains on any given day is $\frac{1}{5}$. In this city, what is the probability that it rains at least one day in three consecutive days?

(A) $\dfrac{60}{125}$ (B) $\dfrac{61}{125}$ (C) $\dfrac{62}{125}$ (D) $\dfrac{63}{125}$ (E) $\dfrac{64}{125}$

Answer (B): First, the probability that it does not rain on any given day is $1 - \frac{1}{5} = \frac{4}{5}$. Next, for three consecutive days, the probability of not having any rain is

$$\left(\frac{4}{5}\right)^3 = \frac{64}{125}.$$

Finally, the probability that it rains at least one day in three consecutive days is

$$1 - \frac{64}{125} = \frac{61}{125}.$$

13. There are 12 teams in a double-elimination tournament, where a team is eliminated when they lose two games. In each game, two teams play and one of them loses. The tournament continues until only one team is left. At most how many games will the

tournament have?

(A) 20 **(B)** 21 **(C)** 22 **(D)** 23 **(E)** 24

Answer (D): To have only 1 team left, 11 teams must be eliminated, each after losing 2 games. This leads to $2 \times 11 = 22$ games. In addition, the last team standing can lose at most 1 game, so the tournament can have at most 23 games.

14. Ayla, Ciana, and Ellen are three siblings. The product of their ages is 192. What is the smallest possible value for the sum of their ages?

(A) 18 **(B)** 19 **(C)** 20 **(D)** 21 **(E)** 22

Answer (A): By trying various possibilities observe that the sum gets smaller as the three numbers get 'closer' to each other. As we try getting the numbers close we get the triple (4,6,8) which gives a sum of 18. To actually show that this is the smallest sum, note that the divisors of 192 that are smaller than 18 are 1, 2, 3, 4, 6, 8, 12, and 16. It is easy to see that if one of the numbers is 12 or 16, the sum of three would be more than 18. If all the numbers are at most 8, then the only possible triplet besides (4,6,8) is (3,8,8) which has a sum of 19. Hence, the answer is 18.

15. Let $\triangle ABC$ be an isosceles triangle with $AB = AC = 6$. P is a point on side BC such that $BP = 3PC$. X is a point on AB such that $\overline{PX} \parallel \overline{CA}$. Y is a point on AC such that $\overline{PY} \parallel \overline{BA}$. What is the perimeter of quadrilateral $AXPY$?

(A) 10 **(B)** 12 **(C)** 15 **(D)** 16 **(E)** 20

Answer (B): Because of parallel lines, $\triangle BXP$ and $\triangle PYC$ are both similar to $\triangle BAC$. It follows that $\triangle BXP$ and $\triangle PYC$ are also isosceles triangles with $XP = XB$ and $PY = CY$. Therefore, the perimeter of $AXPY$ is equal to

$$AX + XP + PY + YA = AX + XB + CY + YA = AB + CA = 6 + 6 = 12.$$

16. Cindy thinks of a positive integer, adds four to it, squares the result, and subtracts 25. For how many starting numbers would Cindy end up with a negative number?

    (A) 0   **(B)** 1   **(C)** 5   **(D)** 9   **(E)** 12

    Answer (A): Let Cindy's number be x. Then the resulting number is

    $$(x + 4)^2 - 25.$$

    For this to be negative we need $(x + 4)^2 < 5^2$ or $-5 < x + 4 < 5$. Subtracting 4 from all the terms we get $-9 < x < 1$. There is no positive integer in this interval so the answer is 0.

17. Sebastian has a bag of eight marbles, five red, and three blue. Without looking, he chooses two marbles from the bag without replacement. What is the probability that at least one of the marbles is blue?

    (A) $\dfrac{1}{3}$ **(B)** $\dfrac{5}{14}$ **(C)** $\dfrac{1}{2}$ **(D)** $\dfrac{9}{14}$ **(E)** $\dfrac{2}{3}$

    Answer (D): We will use complementary counting. The probability that neither marble is blue is the probability that both draws result in a red marble. The first draw has probability $\dfrac{5}{8}$ of being red, and, given that, there are now 4 red marbles in 7, total, so the second draw has probability $\dfrac{4}{7}$ of being red. Therefore, the chance that both draws are red is $\dfrac{5}{8} \times \dfrac{4}{7} = \dfrac{5}{14}$. Finally, the probability that at least one of the marbles is blue is $1 - \dfrac{5}{14} = \dfrac{9}{14}$.

18. A sphere of radius 17 is cut with a plane, leaving it with two pieces with a circular flat side. When one of these pieces is set on a table with the flat side down, it reaches a height of 25 from the table. What is the radius of the circular flat side?

    (A) 12   **(B)** 13   **(C)** 14   **(D)** 15   **(E)** 16

    Answer (D): Let O be the center of the sphere, C be the center of the circular flat side, and P be any point on the circular flat side. Since 25 is more than the radius, 17, the center of the sphere is contained in the piece that was put on the table. OCP

is a right triangle with $OC = 25 - 17 = 8$ and $OP = 17$. Using Pythagorean Theorem we get $CP = \sqrt{17^2 - 8^2} = 15$, which is the radius of the circular flat side.

19. For a positive integer n, let $f(n)$ denote the number of positive factors of n. If the the product

$$f(a) \times f(b) \times f(c)$$

is odd for some distinct positive integers a, b, and c, what is the minimum value of $a + b + c$?

(A) 6   (B) 8   (C) 10   (D) 12   (E) 14

Answer (E): $f(a) \times f(b) \times f(c)$ is odd only if each of $f(a), f(b)$, and $f(c)$ is odd. Moreover, $f(x)$ is odd only when x is a perfect square. Thus, a, b, c must be different positive perfect squares and the minimum sum is $1^2 + 2^2 + 3^2 = 14$.

20. How many real numbers x satisfy

$$\left|2 - |x - 2|\right| + |x + 3| = 5?$$

(A) 0   (B) 1   (C) 2   (D) 4   (E) 6

Answer (C): First note that since the first term, $\left|2 - |x - 2|\right|$, is always non-negative we must have $|x + 3| \le 5$. This implies $x \le 2$. Then,

$$\left|2 - |x - 2|\right| = \left|2 - (2 - x)\right| = |x|.$$

This reduces the original equation to

$$|x| + |x + 3| = 5.$$

When $x > 0$, this gives $2x + 3 = 5$ or $x = 1$.
For $-3 \le x \le 0$, we get $-x + (x + 3) = 3 \neq 5$.
Finally, for $x < -3$, we get $-x + (-x - 3) = -2x - 3 = 5$ or $x = -4$.

We conclude that there are 2 real solutions: -4 and 1.

21. Hasan loves to draw circles on a board and count the number of regions formed. When he draws one circle he gets two regions; inside and outside of the circle. When he draws two circles, he gets at most four regions. When he draws five circles, at most how many regions will he get?

(A) 20   **(B)** 22   **(C)** 26   **(D)** 30   **(E)** 32

Answer (B): We first look for a pattern between the number of intersection points among the circles and the number of regions formed. With one circle, there are 0 points and 2 regions. With two circles, there are 2 points and 4 regions. With three circles, there are 6 points and 8 regions. It looks like the number of regions is always 2 more than the number of intersection points. This is true in general, because every intersection point increases the number of regions by one.

Now, to count the number of intersection points, observe that any two circles can have at most two intersection points. So when five circles are drawn, there will be at most $2 \times \binom{5}{2} = 20$ intersection points. Hence, the largest number of regions formed is $20 + 2 = 22$.

22. In the diagram below, $ABCD$ is a square with side length 4. A circle is inscribed in $ABCD$ and diagonal $\overline{BD}$ intersects the circle at P. What is the length of $\overline{PC}$?

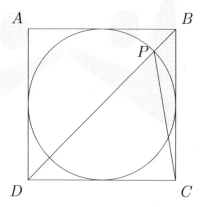

(A) $2\sqrt{3}$ **(B)** $\dfrac{7}{2}$ **(C)** $5 - \sqrt{2}$ **(D)** $2 + \sqrt{3}$ **(E)** $\sqrt{15}$

Answer (A): Let O be the center of the circle which is also the intersection of the diagonals of the square.

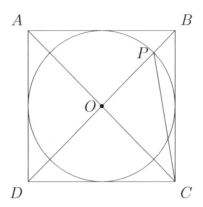

Note that $\angle POC = \angle BOC = 90°$. Looking at the legs of this the right triangle $\triangle POC$, $\overline{PO} = 2$ since it is a radius of the circle, and

$$\overline{CO} = \frac{\overline{AC}}{2} = \frac{2\sqrt{2}}{2} = \sqrt{2}$$

By Pythagorean Theorem,

$$PC^2 = PO^2 + OC^2 = 4 + 8 = 12.$$

We conclude that

$$PC = \sqrt{12} = 2\sqrt{3}.$$

23. In the diagram below, $ABCD$ is a rectangle with $AB = 8$ and $BC = 6$. Points E and F are on $\overline{BD}$ such that $\overline{AE}$ and $\overline{CF}$ are perpendicular to $\overline{BD}$. What is the ratio of the area $AECF$ to the area of $ABCD$?

   (A) $\dfrac{1}{4}$ (B) $\dfrac{7}{25}$ (C) $\dfrac{7}{24}$ (D) $\dfrac{17}{48}$ (E) $\dfrac{13}{24}$

Answer (B): First note that $BC = 10$ by the Pythagorean Theorem.

We consider the area of $AECF$: it is simply twice the area of $\triangle AEF$. So our desired answer is $\dfrac{2 \cdot \dfrac{1}{2} \cdot AE \cdot EF}{48} = \dfrac{AE \cdot EF}{48}$.

Note that $\triangle AED$ is similar to $\triangle BAD$. From this we can find that $\dfrac{AE}{AD} = \dfrac{BA}{BD}$, so $AE = \dfrac{6 \cdot 8}{10} = \dfrac{24}{5}$.

64

Next, we find the length of $\overline{DE}$. By the same similar triangle, $\dfrac{DE}{AD} = \dfrac{AD}{BD}$, so $DE = \dfrac{6 \cdot 6}{10} = \dfrac{18}{5}$. We can now compute EF:

$$EF = BD - ED - FB = BD - 2DE = 10 - 2 \cdot \frac{18}{5} = \frac{14}{5}.$$

Finally, we compute our answer. It is equal to $\dfrac{AE \cdot EF}{48} = \dfrac{1}{48} \cdot \dfrac{24}{5} \cdot \dfrac{14}{5} = \dfrac{7}{25}.$

24. Benjamin finds that a polynomial with degree four has leading coefficient 1 and roots 3, 5, 7, and 9. What is the sum of the coefficients of this polynomial?

(A) 0   (B) 24   (C) 206   (D) 384   (E) 945

Answer (D): Let P be the polynomial. Since it is monic and has degree four with roots 3, 5, 7, and 9, $P(x) = (x-3)(x-5)(x-7)(x-9)$. We could expand this polynomial and sum the coefficients, but there is a quicker method. If we write out this polynomial as $P(x) = a_4x^4 + a_3x^3 + a_2x^2 + a_1x + a_0$ where $a_4, a_3, \ldots, a_0$ are the coefficients, then the sum of the coefficients is $a_4 + a_3 + a_2 + a_1 + a_0$ which is $P(1)$. When we plug in 1 into P, we get $P(1) = (1-3)(1-5)(1-7)(1-9) = (-2) \times (-4) \times (-6) \times (-8) = 384$.

Remark: In general for any polynomial $P(x)$, the sum of its coefficients is $P(1)$.

25. Let N be the largest positive integer whose base-6 and base-11 representations are reverse of each other and neither representation ends in 0. What is the sum of the digits of N when it is written in base 10?

(A) 15   (B) 16   (C) 17   (D) 18   (E) 20

Answer (B): Since the digits are reverse of each other, base-6 and base-11 representations of N must have the same number of digits, say k. Then, N must be at least the smallest k digit number in base 11, which is 11^{k-1}. Also, it must be smaller than the smallest $k+1$ digit number in base 6, which is 6^k. From $11^{k-1} \le N < 6^k$ it follows that $11^{k-1} < 6^k$. Note that $11^3 = 1331$ is larger than $6^4 = 1296$. So, k cannot be 4 or more. To find the largest N, let us try $k = 3$. Let the base-11 representation of N be abc and base-6 representation of N be cba, where $0 \le a, b, c \le 5$. Then $(abc)_{11} = (cba)_6$

implies $121a + 11b + c = 36c + 6b + a$ which simplifies to $120a + 5b = 35c$ or $24a + b = 7c$. Since c is at most 5, a cannot be more than 1. Trying $a = 1$, we get $b = c = 4$ and $N = (144)_{11} = (441)_6 = 169$. So the answer is $1 + 6 + 9 = 16$.

AMC 8 PRACTICE TESTS VOL 1

TEST-4

INSTRUCTIONS

1. This is a twenty-five question multiple choice test. Each question is followed by answers marked A, B, C, D and E. Only one of these is correct.

2. There is no penalty for guessing. Your score is the number of correct answers.

3. Only scratch paper, graph paper, rulers, protractors, and erasers are allowed as aids. Calculators are NOT allowed. No problems on the test *require* the use of a calculator.

4. Figures are not necessarily drawn to scale.

5. You will have **40 minutes** to complete the test.

1. A traffic light cycles between the three colors red, green, and yellow. It is red $\frac{1}{2}$ of the time and green $\frac{2}{5}$ of the time. What fraction of the time is it yellow?

   (A) $\frac{1}{10}$ (B) $\frac{1}{5}$ (C) $\frac{3}{10}$ (D) $\frac{2}{5}$ (E) $\frac{1}{2}$

2. In a shop, coffee costs \$2.50. The owner applies a 30% discount on all items. What is the discounted price of two coffees?

   (A) \$1.50   (B) \$1.75   (C) \$2.25   (D) \$3.00   (E) \$3.50

3. What is the perimeter of a rectangle with length $\frac{2}{5}$ inches and area $\frac{1}{5}$ square inches?

   (A) 0.9 in.   (B) 1.2 in.   (C) 1.5 in.   (D) 1.8 in.   (E) 2.2 in.

4. If 30 pencils are worth 50 staples, and two erasers are worth eight pencils, how many staples are three erasers worth?

   (A) 3   (B) 5   (C) 11   (D) 15   (E) 20

5. Benny puts his money into the stock market. During the first month, it decreases by 20%. During the second month, it increases by 30%. By what percent does his money increase after the two months?

   (A) 2%   (B) 4%   (C) 6%   (D) 8%   (E) 10%

6. When Steve divides his bag of marbles into groups of three, he has one left over. When he divides his marbles into groups of four, he also has one left over. If Steve has at least 2 marbles, what is the smallest possible number of marbles he could have?

   (A) 9   (B) 10   (C) 11   (D) 12   (E) 13

7. One day, 50 fish are caught, tagged, and released back into a lake. On the next day, 200 fish are randomly caught, and it is noted that 20 of them have tags. What is the best estimate for the population of fish in the lake, including the fish that were caught?

   (A) 230   (B) 250   (C) 300   (D) 400   (E) 500

8. Two fair six-sided dice are rolled. What is the probability that the product of the numbers shown is prime?

   (A) $\dfrac{1}{12}$ (B) $\dfrac{1}{9}$ (C) $\dfrac{1}{6}$ (D) $\dfrac{7}{36}$ (E) $\dfrac{1}{3}$

9. How many ways are there to place 4 same checker pieces on a 4×4 board such that no two pieces lie on the same row or column?

   (A) 6   (B) 12   (C) 16   (D) 18   (E) 24

10. The sum of two distinct positive integers is 2020. What is the maximum possible value of their greatest common divisor?

    (A) 2   (B) 20   (C) 101   (D) 505   (E) 1010

11. Buzzy the Bee is trapped in a box with length 12 inches, width 4 inches, and height 3 inches. It is located at one vertex of the box. What is the shortest distance, in inches, Buzzy needs to fly to get to the opposite vertex?

    (A) 5   (B) 12   (C) 13   (D) 16   (E) 19

12. A right triangle has legs of lengths 15 and x, and a hypotenuse of length $x + 1$. What is the perimeter of the triangle?

    (A) 34   (B) 52   (C) 78   (D) 240   (E) 464

13. Alice and Bob start at the same time and place driving in the same direction. Alice drives at a constant speed of 50 mph. Bob drives at 10 mph for the first hour, 20 mph for the second hour, 30 mph for the third hour, and so on, increasing his speed by 10 mph every hour. In how many hours will Bob meet Alice again?

(A) 5   (B) 6   (C) 7   (D) 8   (E) 9

14. From the origin, there is exactly one path to get to the point $(9, 12)$ by first following a line with slope 1 and then following a line with slope -1. What is the length of this path?

(A) $9\sqrt{2}$ (B) 15   (C) $9\sqrt{2} + 3$ (D) $12\sqrt{2}$ (E) 21

15. In the following addition of five-digit numbers, each letter represents a digit (not necessarily distinct). How many possible solutions (A, B, C, D, E, F) are there?

$$\begin{array}{r} ABCDE \\ + \ ACDEF \\ \hline FFFFF \end{array}$$

(A) 0   (B) 1   (C) 4   (D) 8   (E) 16

16. Stephen the Stacker is stacking cubes, one on top of another, to form a tower with height at least one. If he has 6 cubes with side length 6, 5, 4, 3, 2, and 1, how many ways can he stack some or all of the cubes into a tower so that every cube in the tower is smaller than the cube below it?

(A) 1   (B) 6   (C) 63   (D) 120   (E) 720

17. In a soccer league with 10 teams every team plays one game against every other team. The teams are awarded 3 points for a win, 1 point for a tie, and no points for a loss. At the end of the tournament, the sum of the points of all the teams is 127. How many games ended in a tie?

    (A) 8   (B) 10   (C) 12   (D) 14   (E) 16

18. A light is initially off. It has a switch and flipping the switch has one of three possible effects. There is a $\frac{1}{5}$ chance of nothing happening, a $\frac{1}{5}$ chance of short-circuiting the light, meaning it will stay off permanently, and a $\frac{3}{5}$ chance of turning the light on if it is off, and off if it is on. After exactly three flips of the switch, what is the probability that the light will be on?

    (A) $\frac{1}{125}$ (B) $\frac{9}{125}$ (C) $\frac{1}{25}$ (D) $\frac{1}{5}$ (E) $\frac{36}{125}$

19. In the coordinate plane, the four points $(1, 3)$, $(8, 4)$, $(7, 11)$, and $(0, 10)$ form a square. There exists a line passing through point $P(12, 12)$ that divides the square into two regions of equal areas. What is the slope of this line?

    (A) $\frac{7}{16}$ (B) $\frac{1}{2}$ (C) $\frac{9}{16}$ (D) $\frac{5}{8}$ (E) $\frac{11}{16}$

20. Sam chooses a point A on a circle. He draws the vertices of the regular polygon with 60 vertices that are contained on the circle and has one vertex at A, and he also draws the vertices of the regular polygon with 72 vertices that are contained on the circle and has one vertex at A. How many different points are drawn?

    (A) 66   (B) 84   (C) 120   (D) 131   (E) 132

21. A unit cube is colored such that two adjacent faces are blue while the rest of the cube is red. 8 of these cubes are placed together to form a larger cube with side length 2. How many ways are there to orient these 8 unit cubes such that all the faces of the larger cube are entirely red? Rotations and reflections are considered distinct.

    (A) 256   (B) 729   (C) 768   (D) 4096   (E) 6561

22. Let a, b, c be three positive numbers that satisfy $\dfrac{a^2}{a^2+b^2} = \dfrac{1}{10}$ and $\dfrac{b^2}{b^2+c^2} = \dfrac{1}{17}$. What is the value of $\dfrac{c}{c+a}$?

(A) $\dfrac{1}{2}$ (B) $\dfrac{6}{7}$ (C) $\dfrac{10}{11}$ (D) $\dfrac{12}{13}$ (E) $\dfrac{13}{14}$

23. Let ABC be an equilateral triangle with side length 2. Let AD, be the altitude from A to BC, DE be the altitude from D to AB, and DF be the altitude from D to AC. What is the ratio of the area of $AEDF$ to the area of ABC?

(A) $\dfrac{2}{3}$ (B) $\dfrac{3}{4}$ (C) $\dfrac{4}{5}$ (D) $\dfrac{5}{6}$ (E) $\dfrac{8}{9}$

24. The graphs of $y = x^2 - a$ and $x^2 + y^2 = a^2$ intersect at exactly one point. Find the largest possible value of a.

(A) 0 (B) $\dfrac{1}{8}$ (C) $\dfrac{1}{4}$ (D) $\dfrac{1}{2}$ (E) 1

25. Let $N_k = \underbrace{10101\ldots0101}_{k\ 1\text{'s}}$. For example $N_3 = 10101$. What is the smallest positive integer k such that the string "21" appears in N_k^2?

(A) 2 (B) 7 (C) 12 (D) 21 (E) 22

Test-4 Answer Key

1. A
2. E
3. D
4. E
5. B
6. E
7. E
8. C
9. E
10. D
11. C
12. D
13. E
14. D
15. C
16. C
17. A
18. E
19. D
20. C
21. E
22. D
23. B
24. D
25. C

Test-4 Solutions

1. A traffic light cycles between the three colors red, green, and yellow. It is red $\frac{1}{2}$ of the time and green $\frac{2}{5}$ of the time. What fraction of the time is it yellow?

    (A) $\frac{1}{10}$ (B) $\frac{1}{5}$ (C) $\frac{3}{10}$ (D) $\frac{2}{5}$ (E) $\frac{1}{2}$

    Answer (A): The sum of the three frequencies must be 1. Thus, the fraction of the time being yellow is

    $$1 - \left(\frac{2}{5} + \frac{1}{2}\right) = \frac{10}{10} - \left(\frac{4}{10} + \frac{5}{10}\right) = \frac{1}{10}.$$

2. In a shop, coffee costs $2.50. The owner applies a 30% discount on all items. What is the discounted price of two coffees?

    (A) $1.50   (B) $1.75   (C) $2.25   (D) $3.00   (E) $3.50

    Answer (E): The original price of two coffees is $5. After a 30% discount, it becomes

    $$(100\% - 30\%) \times \$5 = \$3.50.$$

3. What is the perimeter of a rectangle with length $\frac{2}{5}$ inches and area $\frac{1}{5}$ square inches?

    (A) 0.9 in.   (B) 1.2 in.   (C) 1.5 in.   (D) 1.8 in.   (E) 2.2 in.

Answer (D): Since the area of a rectangle is the product of its length and width, we find that its width is $\dfrac{1/5}{2/5} = \dfrac{1}{2}$ inches. Hence, the perimeter is

$$2 \times \left(\frac{2}{5} + \frac{1}{2}\right) = 2 \times (0.4 + 0.5) = 1.8 \text{ in.}$$

4. If 30 pencils are worth 50 staples, and two erasers are worth eight pencils, how many staples are three erasers worth?

(A) 3   **(B)** 5   **(C)** 11   **(D)** 15   **(E)** 20

Answer (E): If 2 erasers are worth 8 pencils, then 1 eraser is worth 4 pencils and 3 erasers are worth $4 \times 3 = 12$ pencils. Also, if 30 pencils are worth 50 staples, then 3 pencils are worth 5 staples, so $3 \times 4 = 12$ pencils are worth $5 \times 4 = 20$ staples. Thus, if 3 erasers are worth 12 pencils, and 12 pencils are worth 20 staples, then 3 erasers are worth 20 staples.

5. Benny puts his money into the stock market. During the first month, it decreases by 20%. During the second month, it increases by 30%. By what percent does his money increase after the two months?

(A) 2%   **(B)** 4%   **(C)** 6%   **(D)** 8%   **(E)** 10%

Answer (B): The losses during the first month is 20%, and Benny is left with 80% of his investment. The earnings during the second month is 30% of the 80% which is 24%, increasing the percentage to $80\% + 24\% = 104\%$. Thus, after two months, his money increased by 4%.

6. When Steve divides his bag of marbles into groups of three, he has one left over. When he divides his marbles into groups of four, he also has one left over. If Steve has at least 2 marbles, what is the smallest possible number of marbles he could have?

(A) 9   **(B)** 10   **(C)** 11   **(D)** 12   **(E)** 13

Answer (E): Leaving 1 marble aside, the number of the remaining marbles, which is at least 1, must be a multiple of 3 and 4; hence, it is a multiple of 12. The smallest positive multiple of 12 is 12 itself and adding the marble left aside, we get 13 marbles.

7. One day, 50 fish are caught, tagged, and released back into a lake. On the next day, 200 fish are randomly caught, and it is noted that 20 of them have tags. What is the best estimate for the population of fish in the lake, including the fish that were caught?

(A) 230   (B) 250   (C) 300   (D) 400   (E) 500

Answer (E): Among the fish caught on the 2nd day, 10% have tags. Based on this, we estimate that 10% of the fish in the lake have tags. Hence, the number of fish can be estimated to be 10 times the number of those with tags, or $10 \times 50 = 500$.

8. Two fair six-sided dice are rolled. What is the probability that the product of the numbers shown is prime?

(A) $\dfrac{1}{12}$ (B) $\dfrac{1}{9}$ (C) $\dfrac{1}{6}$ (D) $\dfrac{7}{36}$ (E) $\dfrac{1}{3}$

Answer (C): To have a product that is prime one of the numbers must be 1 and the other must be $2, 3,$ or 5. Hence, there are 6 pairs that work: $(1, 2), (1, 3), (1, 5), (2, 1), (3, 1), (5, 1)$. Since there are $6 \times 6 = 36$ possibilities, the answer is $\dfrac{6}{36} = \dfrac{1}{6}$.

9. How many ways are there to place 4 same checker pieces on a 4×4 board such that no two pieces lie on the same row or column?

(A) 6   (B) 12   (C) 16   (D) 18   (E) 24

Answer (E): Since we have exactly 4 pieces and 4 rows, and no row can contain 2 pieces each row must contain exactly one piece. Similarly, each column must contain exactly one piece. Going in rows from top to bottom, there are 4 ways to choose the piece on the first row, 3 ways left for the second row, 2 ways for the third row, and only 1 way for the fourth row. Hence, the answer is $4 \times 3 \times 2 \times 1 = 24$.

10. The sum of two distinct positive integers is 2020. What is the maximum possible value of their greatest common divisor?

(A) 2   **(B)** 20   **(C)** 101   **(D)** 505   **(E)** 1010

Answer (D): Let the greatest common divisor of the two numbers be g. Since g divides both numbers, it also divides their sum, 2020. The smallest few divisors of 2020 are $1, 2, 4, 5, \ldots$; hence, its largest divisors are

$$\frac{2020}{1}, \frac{2020}{2}, \frac{2020}{4}, \frac{2020}{5}, \ldots$$

If g were 2020, since each number is a multiple of g, the sum would be more than 2020. If g were 1010, the two distinct numbers would be at least 1010 and 2020, and their sum would also be more than 2020. If g is the next largest candidate, 505, the two numbers can be 505 and 1515. Hence, the answer is 505.

11. Buzzy the Bee is trapped in a box with length 12 inches, width 4 inches, and height 3 inches. It is located at one vertex of the box. What is the shortest distance, in inches, Buzzy needs to fly to get to the opposite vertex?

(A) 5   **(B)** 12   **(C)** 13   **(D)** 16   **(E)** 19

Answer (C): The shortest possible distance between two opposite vertices is given by the space diagonal, which has length

$$\sqrt{3^2 + 4^2 + 12^2} = \sqrt{169} = 13.$$

12. A right triangle has legs of lengths 15 and x, and a hypotenuse of length $x + 1$. What is the perimeter of the triangle?

(A) 34   **(B)** 52   **(C)** 78   **(D)** 240   **(E)** 464

Answer (D): By the Pythagorean Theorem, we have that $15^2 + x^2 = (x + 1)^2$. Simplifying, we get that $2x + 1 = 225$, or $x = 112$. Hence, the sides of our triangle are $15, 112, 113$, so our answer is $15 + 112 + 113 = 240$.

Alternatively, note that the perimeter of the triangle is $15 + x + (x+1) = 15 + (2x+1)$, so as soon as we find $2x + 1 = 225$ we can plug it in to get the answer $15 + 225 = 240$.

13. Alice and Bob start at the same time and place driving in the same direction. Alice drives at a constant speed of 50 mph. Bob drives at 10 mph for the first hour, 20 mph for the second hour, 30 mph for the third hour, and so on, increasing his speed by 10 mph every hour. In how many hours will Bob meet Alice again?

    (A) 5   **(B)** 6   **(C)** 7   **(D)** 8   **(E)** 9

    Answer (E): When Bob meets Alice, they would have covered the same distances in the same amount of times, so their average speeds would be the same. Alice's average speed is 50 mph. Bob's average speed is the average of his hourly average speeds $10, 20, 30, \ldots$ This is an arithmetic sequence and hence the average is the average of the first and last terms. From this we find that his hourly average speed for the last hour before meeting Alice has to be 90 mph and it will take them 9 hours to meet again.

14. From the origin, there is exactly one path to get to the point $(9, 12)$ by first following a line with slope 1 and then following a line with slope -1. What is the length of this path?

    (A) $9\sqrt{2}$ **(B)** 15   **(C)** $9\sqrt{2} + 3$ **(D)** $12\sqrt{2}$ **(E)** 21

    Answer (D): By following a line with slope 1, one may reach the point (r, r) for some real number r. We want to be able to reach $(9, 12)$ from this point, so we want the line connecting (r, r) to $(9, 12)$ to have slope -1:

    $$\frac{r - 12}{r - 9} = -1$$
    $$r - 12 = 9 - r$$
    $$r = 10.5.$$

    Therefore, the length of the path is the sum of the lengths from $(0, 0)$ to $(10.5, 10.5)$ and from $(10.5, 10.5)$ to $(9, 12)$, or $10.5\sqrt{2} + 1.5\sqrt{2} = 12\sqrt{2}$.

    Alternatively, let O be the origin, $P = (9, 12)$, Q be the projection of (the foot of the altitude from) P onto the line $y = x$, and $R = (12, 12)$. Note that the path in question is $O \rightarrow Q \rightarrow P$ with length $OQ + QP$ but since QPR is an isosceles right triangle, $OQ = QR$ and we get $OQ + QR = OR = 12\sqrt{2}$.

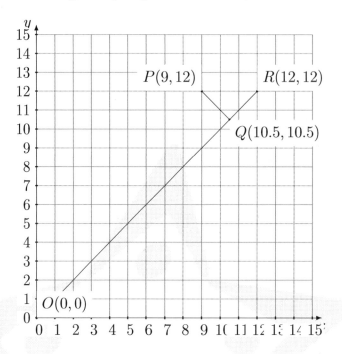

15. In the following addition of five-digit numbers, each letter represents a digit (not necessarily distinct). How many possible solutions (A, B, C, D, E, F) are there?

$$\begin{array}{r} ABCDE \\ + \ ACDEF \\ \hline FFFFF \end{array}$$

(A) 0   **(B)** 1   **(C)** 4   **(D)** 8   **(E)** 16

Answer (C): First, we look at the units digits: $E + F = F$ so $E = 0$. Next, we look at the tens digits: $D + E = D + 0 = F$, so $D = F$. Continuing in this fashion, we find that $C = 0$, $B = F$, and $F = 2A$. Hence,

$$(A, B, C, D, E, F) = (A, 2A, 0, 2A, 0, 2A).$$

Since A is positive and $F = 2A$ is also a digit, possible A values are 1, 2, 3, and 4, giving 4 solutions.

16. Stephen the Stacker is stacking cubes, one on top of another, to form a tower with height at least one. If he has 6 cubes with side length 6, 5, 4, 3, 2, and 1, how many ways can he stack some or all of the cubes into a tower so that every cube in the tower is smaller than the cube below it?

(A) 1 **(B)** 6 **(C)** 63 **(D)** 120 **(E)** 720

Answer (C): Let us start with a full tower with all 6 blocks. For each block, we can either keep it or remove it. If the block is removed, all the other blocks above are moved down. Thus, the number of ways to make this tower is $2^6 = 64$, but we must subtract 1 for the case where we remove every block, since then there is no tower at all, giving 63.

17. In a soccer league with 10 teams every team plays one game against every other team. The teams are awarded 3 points for a win, 1 point for a tie, and no points for a loss. At the end of the tournament, the sum of the points of all the teams is 127. How many games ended in a tie?

(A) 8 **(B)** 10 **(C)** 12 **(D)** 14 **(E)** 16

Answer (A): Note that a a non-tie game adds $3 + 0 = 3$ points to the total point count across all teams, while a tie game adds $1 + 1 = 2$ points.

There are $\binom{10}{2} = 45$ games played in the tournament. If no games end in a tie, a total of $3 \times 45 = 135$ points would be rewarded. The actual number of rewarded points is 8 less than this. Every time a game ends in a tie, 1 less point (relative to a non-tie game) is rewarded. So, there must be 8 games which ended in a tie.

18. A light is initially off. It has a switch and flipping the switch has one of three possible effects. There is a $\frac{1}{5}$ chance of nothing happening, a $\frac{1}{5}$ chance of short-circuiting the light, meaning it will stay off permanently, and a $\frac{3}{5}$ chance of turning the light on if it is off, and off if it is on. After exactly three flips of the switch, what is the probability that the light will be on?

(A) $\dfrac{1}{125}$ **(B)** $\dfrac{9}{125}$ **(C)** $\dfrac{1}{25}$ **(D)** $\dfrac{1}{5}$ **(E)** $\dfrac{36}{125}$

Answer (E): Let $*$ denote that nothing happens, with a $\dfrac{1}{5}$ chance and let S denote that the light is switched, with a $\dfrac{3}{5}$ chance. Note that if at any point the light short-circuits, it will never be on at the end. We need an odd number of S's to ensure that the light is on at the end. Thus, the ways this can happen are SSS, $S**$, $*S*$, and $**S$, which have probabilities $\dfrac{27}{125}$, $\dfrac{3}{125}$, $\dfrac{3}{125}$, and $\dfrac{3}{125}$, respectively. Thus, the total probability is $\dfrac{36}{125}$.

19. In the coordinate plane, the four points $(1,3)$, $(8,4)$, $(7,11)$, and $(0,10)$ form a square. There exists a line passing through point $P(12,12)$ that divides the square into two regions of equal areas. What is the slope of this line?

    (A) $\dfrac{7}{16}$ **(B)** $\dfrac{1}{2}$ **(C)** $\dfrac{9}{16}$ **(D)** $\dfrac{5}{8}$ **(E)** $\dfrac{11}{16}$

    Answer (D): By symmetry any line that passes through the center of the square divides the square into two equal areas. The center of the square is the midpoint of either diagonal so we can compute its coordinates as

    $$\left(\frac{1+7}{2}, \frac{3+11}{2}\right) = \left(\frac{8+0}{2}, \frac{4+10}{2}\right) = (4,7).$$

    The slope of the line passing through $P(12,12)$ and the center $(4,7)$ is $\dfrac{12-7}{12-4} = \dfrac{5}{8}$.

20. Sam chooses a point A on a circle. He draws the vertices of the regular polygon with 60 vertices that are contained on the circle and has one vertex at A, and he also draws the vertices of the regular polygon with 72 vertices that are contained on the circle and has one vertex at A. How many different points are drawn?

    (A) 66   **(B)** 84   **(C)** 120   **(D)** 131   **(E)** 132

    Answer (C): There are a total of $60 + 72 = 132$ points, but some of them overlap. Specifically, a position that is r points clockwise from A (with respect to the set of 60 points) is equal to a position that is s points clockwise from A (with respect to the set of 72 points) if and only if $\dfrac{r}{60} = \dfrac{s}{72}$, or $\dfrac{r}{5} = \dfrac{s}{6}$. We are looking for integer solutions of this when $0 \le r < 60$ and $0 \le s < 72$. Clearly, the first solution is $(r, s) = (0, 0)$ (the point A), and all solutions are of the form $(5k, 6k)$ for an integer $0 \le k < 12$. There are 12 points that were counted twice. Therefore, the number of different points is $132 - 12 = 120$.

Remark: This may be generalized to any number of sets of points of size a and b: The number of distinct points on the circle is $a + b - \gcd(a, b)$.

21. A unit cube is colored such that two adjacent faces are blue while the rest of the cube is red. 8 of these cubes are placed together to form a larger cube with side length 2. How many ways are there to orient these 8 unit cubes such that all the faces of the larger cube are entirely red? Rotations and reflections are considered distinct.

    (A) 256   **(B)** 729   **(C)** 768   **(D)** 4096   **(E)** 6561

    Answer (E): For each unit cube, 3 of the red faces must lie on the exterior of the larger cube. Since there are a total of 4 red faces, each small cube has one red face in the interior of the larger cube. Each unit cube has 3 faces in the larger cube's interior, so this makes 3 possible orientations for each unit cube. Thus, the total number of ways is $3^8 = 6561$.

22. Let a, b, c be three positive numbers that satisfy $\dfrac{a^2}{a^2 + b^2} = \dfrac{1}{10}$ and $\dfrac{b^2}{b^2 + c^2} = \dfrac{1}{17}$. What is the value of $\dfrac{c}{c + a}$?

    (A) $\dfrac{1}{2}$ **(B)** $\dfrac{6}{7}$ **(C)** $\dfrac{10}{11}$ **(D)** $\dfrac{12}{13}$ **(E)** $\dfrac{13}{14}$

    Answer (D): If $\dfrac{a^2}{a^2 + b^2} = \dfrac{1}{10}$, then by expanding, we have $10a^2 = a^2 + b^2$, or $b^2 = 9a^2$. From this, we get $b = 3a$ since a and b are both positive. Similarly, from the second equation, we have $c^2 = 16b^2$, or $c = 4b$. This means $c = 12a$, so $\dfrac{c}{c + a} = \dfrac{12}{13}$.

23. Let ABC be an equilateral triangle with side length 2. Let AD, be the altitude from A to BC, DE be the altitude from D to AB, and DF be the altitude from D to AC. What is the ratio of the area of $AEDF$ to the area of ABC?

(A) $\dfrac{2}{3}$　　**(B)** $\dfrac{3}{4}$　　**(C)** $\dfrac{4}{5}$　　**(D)** $\dfrac{5}{6}$　　**(E)** $\dfrac{8}{9}$

Answer (B): Because the triangle is symmetric about $\overline{AD}$, the ratio of the area of quadrilateral $AEDF$ to the area of $\triangle ABC$ is equal to the ratio of the area of $\triangle AED$ to the area of $\triangle ABD$, which is then equal to the ratio of AE to AB since the two triangles share common height $\overline{DE}$. Letting $a = BC$, we find that $BD = \dfrac{BC}{2} = \dfrac{a}{2}$, $BE = \dfrac{BD}{2} = \dfrac{a}{4}$ and $AE = AB - BE = \dfrac{3a}{4}$. Hence,

$$\frac{AE}{AB} = \frac{3a/4}{a} = \frac{3}{4}.$$

24. The graphs of $y = x^2 - a$ and $x^2 + y^2 = a^2$ intersect at exactly one point. Find the largest possible value of a.

(A) 0　　**(B)** $\dfrac{1}{8}$　　**(C)** $\dfrac{1}{4}$　　**(D)** $\dfrac{1}{2}$　　**(E)** 1

Answer (D): When two graphs intersect at some point (x, y), (x, y) must be a solution to both equations. Since $(x, y) = (0, -a)$ is a solution to the system of equations it must be the unique solution. The first equation gives $x^2 = y + a$. Plugging this into the second equation, we get $y^2 + y + a - a^2 = (y + a)(y - a + 1) = 0$. This gives solutions $y = -a$ and $y = a - 1$ which then gives $x^2 = y + a = 0$ or $2a - 1$. Since the unique solution to the system has $x = 0$, $x^2 = 2a - 1$ cannot give another solution. It follows that $2a - 1 \le 0$ and $a \le \dfrac{1}{2}$.

Finally, when $a = \dfrac{1}{2}$, we get $x^2 = y + \dfrac{1}{2}$ and $\dfrac{1}{4} = x^2 + y^2 = y^2 + y + \dfrac{1}{2}$. Solving this quadratic equation in y, we find that there is a unique solution $y = -\dfrac{1}{2}$, which gives $x = 0$. So $a = \dfrac{1}{2}$ indeed works and is the largest possible value.

25. Let $N_k = \underbrace{10101\ldots0101}_{k\ 1\text{'s}}$. For example $N_3 = 10101$. What is the smallest positive integer k such that the string "21" appears in N_k^2?

(A) 2 **(B)** 7 **(C)** 12 **(D)** 21 **(E)** 22

Answer (C): We begin by experimenting with squaring N_k's. We can compute that $N_1^2 = 1$, $N_2^2 = 10201$, $N_3^2 = 102030201$, etc. We find that the square of N_k is simply the ordered list of the numbers from 1 to k then back to 1, with each number written as a block of 2 digits - e.g. 7 is written as "07". None of the squares N_1^2 through N_9^2 contain the string "21" because non-zero digits are all separated from one another by zeroes. Going forward to N_{10}^2 and N_{11}^2 we are adding strings "10" and "11" in the middle of the number but none of these lead to a "21" string. On the other hand, N_{12}^2 contains a "21" string within the part

$$\ldots 11\,12\,11 \ldots$$

Therefore, the answer is 12.

Made in the USA
Las Vegas, NV
12 November 2024

11704703R00052